Understanding and Teaching the At-Risk Adult Student

Strategies to Improve Retention and Success

Diane Mierzwik

ROWMAN & LITTLEFIELD EDUCATION
A division of
ROWMAN & LITTLEFIELD PUBLISHERS, INC.
Lanham • New York • Toronto • Plymouth, UK

Published by Rowman & Littlefield Education
A division of Rowman & Littlefield Publishers, Inc.
A wholly owned subsidary of The Rowman & Littlefield Publishing Group, Inc.
4501 Forbes Boulevard, Suite 200, Lanham, Maryland 20706
www.rowman.com

10 Thornbury Road, Plymouth PL6 7PP, United Kingdom

This book was placed by the Educational Design Services LLC literary agency

British Library Cataloguing in Publication Information Available

Library of Congress Cataloging-in-Publication Data

Mierzwik, Diane.
Understanding and teaching the at-risk adult student : strategies to improve retention and success /
Diane Mierzwik.
pages cm
Includes bibliographical references and index.
ISBN 978-1-4758-0164-4 (cloth : alk. paper)—ISBN 978-1-4758-0165-1 (pbk. : alk. paper)—ISBN
978-1-4758-0166-8 (electronic)
1. Learning disabled—Education—United States. I. Title.
LC4818.M54 2013
371.90973—dc23
2012046146

™
The paper used in this publication meets the minimum requirements of American
National Standard for Information Sciences Permanence of Paper for Printed Library
Materials, ANSI/NISO Z39.48-1992.

Printed in the United States of America

Contents

Preface   v

Acknowledgments   vii

Introduction   ix

1   Defining "At Risk"   1

2   Undiagnosed Learning Disabilities and Behavioral
    Disorders   9

3   Substance Abuse–Induced Brain Dysfunction   21

4   Chronic Criminogenic Behaviors   27

5   The Adult Brain   35

6   Managing the At-Risk Adult Learner   43

7   Classroom Environment   57

8   Delivery of New Materials   67

9   Explicit Teaching of Problem-Solving Skills   81

10 The Use of Graphic Organizers and Other Nontraditional
    Teaching Strategies   89

11 Group Processing and Cooperative Learning Strategies   99

Index   107

About the Author   113

Preface

When I announced that I was leaving my middle school teaching position for a job working in parolee education, the first thing my colleagues asked was, "Aren't you scared?"

I laughed nervously. Did they know something I didn't?

I thought the transition would be simple. After all, I knew a few things about the parolee population.

I knew I was actually safer teaching in a correctional setting than in a public school setting. Parole officers were right outside my classroom door to support my efforts, and to ensure my safety there were people with weapons and consequences that were measurable and definite.

I knew most people on parole had a substance use disorder and that the inappropriate use of substances halts emotional and intellectual development when the use begins, usually in middle school. So, developmentally, my adult students would be middle school students.

I believed most people on parole had served time for a felony and had been released because of our society's belief that after having served time, parolees could choose to rejoin society in productive, meaningful ways. They just needed to be given an opportunity with the proper tools. Well, this was right—to a certain extent.

What I didn't know was that though my students might be emotionally and intellectually adolescents, as long as they continued to use drugs and repeat unhealthy habits, their ability to grow developmentally would remain stuck, no matter what I did.

What I didn't know was that no matter how many tools I gave students for success, whether they were tools for healthy living or tools to write an effective cover letter and resume for a job search, some students would refuse to put these tools to good use and would repeat the same behavior that got them in trouble in the first place.

I learned that teaching at-risk adults is a unique experience. Each student faced distinctive challenges because of his or her past and choices, and I had to ensure that each one had the opportunity to be successful.

For those of us teaching at-risk adult students, meeting this challenge is imperative. Even adult educators not specifically teaching in prisons, jails, or rehabilitation centers must meet the needs of this population, for they are increasingly showing up in all adult education classrooms.

The National Center for Education Statistics reported in 2005 that 92 million adults—44 percent of the U.S. population—participated in some form of adult education. Some 60 million of these people were involved in education other than college.

The Bureau of Justice Statistics reported in 2006 that 7.2 million adults were under the supervision of the nation's criminal justice system. Of this number, 2 million were incarcerated, 4.2 million were on probation, and 1 million were on parole.

Many state correctional agencies are now adding the term *rehabilitation* to their names. In 2005, California changed the name from California Department of Corrections to California Department of Corrections and *Rehabilitation*. The nation's focus on rehabilitation comes after decades of "tough sentencing" laws and few programs. That focus resulted in a surge in the population of men and women who are incarcerated, on parole, or on probation. These adults are returning to the classroom, seeking education as a means to reenter society.

The need to prepare teachers to face the challenges of working with this unique population is growing as school districts contract out to provide classes in jails, in prisons, and in probation and parole offices.

My hope is this book will provide trainers of teachers, teachers, and teachers in training an overview of the population they will be serving; offer research on the unique challenges these students present, including undiagnosed learning disabilities, substance abuse brain dysfunction, criminogenic behaviors, and adult learner challenges; as well as provide the reader with evidence-based strategies including class management techniques, instructional strategies, and teacher-student relations guidelines.

There are over 1 million educators of adults who are teaching at-risk adults in their on-the-job training, in their college classrooms, and in adult schools across the country. I'm sure they are also faced with many tough questions, not the least of which is "Aren't you afraid?" A better question is "How are you successful with those students?" This book is an attempt to begin to answer that question.

Acknowledgments

This book would not have been possible without the support from so many people.

I'd like to thank Laura Strachan, Mary Lou Browning, and Shannon Swain for introducing me to the fascinating field of correctional education. I'd like to thank Tom Qualye for involving me in writing curriculum for the field. I'd like to thank my agent, Bertram Linder, for finding a home for the manuscript.

Thanks goes out to Scott McClure and Debbie Smith for their invaluable feedback on the manuscript and to Lindsey Schauer and Carlie Wall for their careful attention to the final product.

Finally, thanks to all the professional educators whose work often goes unnoticed and undervalued.

Introduction

"You can't make excuses for these students," the presenter at the Correctional Educators Association's annual conference stated. After watching many in the audience squirm uncomfortably in their seats, she continued. "But it is important to acknowledge the reasons for their situations."

I had a difficult time listening to the rest of the presentation as I mulled over the difference between making excuses and understanding reasons.

I thought of the students I worked with. I thought of Pops, an elderly man who had severe learning disabilities that were never addressed while he was in public education. He explains that he turned to crime because he couldn't get a job without being able to read and write. I thought of Chris, a young man who grew up with a drug-addicted mother and eventually followed in her footsteps, turning to drugs then committing crimes while under the influence. I thought of Sheryl, an older woman who had run with bikers until she was no longer "desirable" and who was now floundering to make a new life beyond drugs and gangs. Other faces and names and stories floated through my head as I wondered, did knowing their stories allow me to excuse their crimes and their classroom behavior, or did they help me to understand the reasons and therefore be more thoughtful about my approach to teaching them?

I also thought of how often I did not want to know student stories. If I maintained my professional distance, I thought, I would be better able to analyze a student's educational difficulties and make accommodations within the classroom. I thought that without my emotions involved, I was better at my job.

I also recognized that there was a difference between knowing a student's story and understanding the challenges he or she has overcome and those challenges he or she is still facing.

I thought of my own experiences as a student in school. School had always been easy for me, so I might have grown up assuming that if a student was trying, school would be easy for her too. Except I had siblings who struggled in school and despite trying hard, school was always difficult for them. Luckily, they had a stable home life and supportive parents. They are successful adults now. Most of the students I worked with had neither a stable home life nor supportive parents while growing up.

I wondered what it meant for the students I worked with to have struggled in school and to combine that with a criminal record. I accepted my students had made poor choices. I wondered how I could help them make good choices for their future.

I believed the first step would be to understand the reasons for their past failures and to then provide an environment where they could avoid making the same mistakes and could experience success. The learning environment I wanted to create for my students needed to be different from the traditional school experience since that experience had failed them.

This book is organized to help other educators understand the reasons for an at-risk student's past failures and current struggles and to provide strategies for creating a learning environment that allows success for them.

The first part of this book defines "at-risk" as it applies to students in a learning environment and explains the challenges these students face: undiagnosed learning disabilities and behavioral disorders, substance abuse–induced brain dysfunction, chronic criminogenic behaviors, and an aging brain.

The second part of the book provides evidence-based strategies for teaching the at-risk student. These include strategies for managing the at-risk adult learner, creating a safe learning environment, introducing new concepts, explicitly teaching problem-solving skills, using graphic organizers and other nontraditional teaching strategies, and introducing group processing and cooperative learning strategies in the class.

As educators, our job is to provide opportunities for all students to grow as intellectual citizens. Understanding the reasons students are at risk of failing again in the classroom and finding strategies to prevent that failure are key to creating a future full of positive possibilities for students.

As a teacher, I am not interested in excusing my students' failures. I am interested in understanding the reasons for their failures so I can avoid those same failures in my classroom.

ONE

Defining "At Risk"

Many adult education teachers find themselves in the classroom unexpectedly. They get "casually" involved in working with a population of people who are generally disenfranchised from education and the educational system, who are usually living on the outskirts of mainstream society, and who are often seen as a public safety concern, not a person in need of services.[1]

One teacher explains that he was between his bachelor's degree and beginning his master's degree when he came across an advertisement for the teaching position and applied. He's been teaching adults in a literacy program at a parole site for nine years. Another teacher was teaching at the local adult school but needed more hours and found out about the opportunities to teach in the prison for a higher hourly wage, more hours, and full benefits.

Another teacher shared that he likes to teach this unique population because "Any one of them could have been me." He feels an affinity for the students because he had a similar background but found a way out of the lifestyle he was raised in. Still other teachers transition from the traditional K-12 experience or enter teaching adults after making a career change. For the most part, when professionals find themselves teaching adults, they find it isn't much different from other teaching experiences.

Whether teaching at-risk adults was a conscious choice or a casual one, teachers quickly learn that classroom management, good teaching techniques, and evidence-based instructional practices are just as important with adult students as they are with any other group of students.

At the beginning of the semester in one classroom, Lorenzo was consistently off-task. When it was independent practice time, he grabbed the Nerf ball from the teacher's front table and played with it until asked to put it back—then he acted wounded. During class discussion, he always

1

raised his hand to participate, but when called on he asked questions like, "Can I use the restroom?" or "When is break?" He began every class session asking how many days were left.

The teacher assured Lorenzo over and over that the class would go by faster if he focused more on completing each assignment rather than how many class sessions he had left. During class the teacher redirected Lorenzo's off-task behavior and was sure to praise any time on-task. At the end of each class, Lorenzo was the first out the door, often leaving stray papers and supplies in his area for the teacher to pick up.

Lorenzo took up so much of the teacher's energy, she wondered if she should counsel him to drop the class. She decided against it, mostly because she often wondered if he would even make it to the next class.

Lorenzo did make it to the next class and the next and the next. An unexpected thing happened over the course of the semester; Lorenzo turned into a star pupil.

First he began to offer to read aloud when reviewing materials. He started to join in class discussions just when it became obvious that without student input the lesson would not be effective. He offered elucidating personal anecdotes of his own that grounded curricular concepts in personal experience and made the concept clear for the other students. He helped round up students at the end of breaks. He cleared the whiteboard at the end of class. On the last day of class, the teacher realized she was going to miss Lorenzo.

Lorenzo insisted on giving a speech to the other students about how resistant he had been to the information and tools provided in class, but now he got it. He also gave the teacher a handwritten thank you card. Teachers in adult education with at-risk students return again and again to experiences like that with Lorenzo. They remind all educators that recalcitrant students will surprise you in positive ways when given time.

Just as there is a wide variety of teachers and reasons why they are teaching at-risk adults, there is a wide variety of students and stories of how they became at risk.

Typically the term "at risk" is defined as a student who has had life situations that prevented him or her from attaining a socially acceptable lifestyle. Being "at risk" implies a worrisome likelihood of incarceration.[2] At-risk students include those who never graduated from high school, come from a background of poverty, have a criminal record for being involved with gangs and violence, have been identified as having a mental illness, have engaged in substance abuse, or have other social barriers preventing them from attaining acceptable social standing in larger society.

DEMOGRAPHICS OF POPULATION INVOLVED WITH THE CRIMINAL JUSTICE CENTER

Many adult education positions put teachers in daily, direct contact with students who are on the wrong side of the law. In these classrooms there are no identifiers for who committed what crime. Most teachers prefer not to know, seeing their role as redefining their students, not perpetuating the past.

Students who are in prison, in jail, or on probation or parole are at risk because of their criminal record. The Bureau of Justice Statistics has identified common attributes shared by inmates that make it difficult for them to integrate into society in a socially acceptable manner. The population of inmates is mostly male, minority, and young; 65 percent never graduated from high school, 53 percent earned an income below the poverty line; 63 percent committed their crime while under the influence of drugs or alcohol; and 94 percent were convicted of committing a violent offense.

When examining the background of students with a criminal record, several factors put them at risk even before they committed a crime. Some 74 percent of inmates lived either in a single-parent household, with a relative not their parents, or in a foster home, agency, or other institution; 25 percent had parents who abused drugs or alcohol; and 37 percent had an immediate family member with a jail or prison record.[3]

With these alarming statistics one might understand that having come from a disadvantaged background, or being at risk as a child, created a situation that seemed hopeless and promoted socially unacceptable means of survival.

The last alarming statistic is the reason it is so important for educators to continue to provide education to this unique population: these students are parents to more the 826,000 children under the age of eighteen.[4]

Most often a student's children are their last hope. They will bring pictures out of their wallets to show the teacher or have those pictures prominently displayed in their folders. Students' children represent to them the same thing everyone's children represent: a wish for a better future. Often students will tell teachers they have returned to school for their children.

LEARNING DISABILITIES

"Pops" comes to the Computerized Literacy Learning Center three days a week and works in Ultimate Phonics. He's fifty-eight years old and has been in and out of prison since he was nineteen. When he was in school, there were very few programs for "slow learners," as he calls himself.

The teacher's guess is that he has a severe form of dyslexia and auditory-processing problems. Pops is learning to read.

More importantly, while in class, he has found a part-time job because he is finally able to read a job application and fill it out correctly. Pops will soon be released from parole for the first time since his involvement with the criminal system at the age of fourteen. It looks like he may finally have a future. Though Pops was required to come to class by his parole agent, he now comes with a smile on his face and works diligently during the time he is there. He is experiencing success within a supportive environment.

Many adults, like Pops, come to the classroom reluctantly because of past school failures. They may have had negative experiences ranging from receiving poor grades to being humiliated by a misguided teacher.

Many adult students now want to earn a GED or high school diploma but are afraid of the past school failure repeating itself. Some students are aware of a learning disability they have which was diagnosed during school, but because of the lack of a proper support system, they failed in school despite the diagnosis.

Many others were never diagnosed with a disability, but to the keen eye of an adult educator, the disability clearly presents itself in the student's performance. Many of these students often had poor attendance or simply opted out of school before the school could even attempt to help them.

Learning disabilities do not go away as a person matures, and people do not grow out of a learning disability when they become adults.[5] In fact, when adults return to education, it may be the first time they are told they may have a learning disability. Of the 1.5 million students involved in education through the state prisons, 57 percent of them were diagnosed with some form of disability that could interfere with their success in the classroom.[6]

When at-risk students also have a learning disability, their risk is intensified. In addition to struggling with school, they may come from a chaotic home environment and have no one to act as educational advocates for them; subsequently they may have dropped out of school or become involved in substance abuse and crime as a way to escape. What a relief for these students to finally be told that their struggles in school were due to a disability rather than because of laziness, a terrible home life, or being a "bad seed."[7]

Teachers working with these adults have an opportunity to provide strategies and scaffolding to promote success within academic endeavors. A student who is told that his or her past failures were due to a learning disability is relieved of the shame associated with those failures. Providing this student with appropriate tools and opportunities to be successful can encourage the student to reengage in the learning process.

MENTAL ILLNESS

Many of our students are antisocial because of their choices to abuse drugs and commit crimes. But a large number of returning adult students have a mental illness.

According to a study released by the Justice Department in September of 2006, 56 percent of jail inmates in state prisons and 64 percent of inmates across the country reported mental health problems within the past year.[8]

Prisons and jails have become the new mental institutions. Beginning in the 1990s, the mentally ill were moved out of mental hospitals since many mental hospitals operated in poor conditions. Practitioners believed patients could manage their illness outside of direct supervision with the new medications available. In addition to these factors, by deinstitutionalizing these individuals the federal and state systems could cut costs.[9]

Unfortunately, instead of finding new support systems to help manage their mental illness, these individuals survived through committing crimes, often chose to self-medicate with street drugs, ended up in the criminal justice system, and are now in classrooms. The result of deinstitutionalizing the mentally ill has been the incarceration of them, a new form of institutionalization.

As a teacher of these students, it is tempting to want to become the students' advocate, to feel impotent as the educator, and to suggest the students belong somewhere other than the classroom. But the truth is that students who suffer from mental illness often benefit from having a safe, predictable environment. Knowing this allows teachers to provide appropriate curriculum for them.

Silvano, who has autism, comes to class consistently, working slowly through his assigned curriculum. Some days he is able to focus and accomplish much. Other days he stares into space, paces in the classroom, or writes the same word over and over. His teacher has approached Silvano's probation officer to suggest another placement, but there are no other places that ensure that Silvano takes his medications, administered on site by the outpatient medical personnel, and ensure he makes his therapy appointments, also held in the same building as the classroom. The teacher had to learn to accept what is possible with Silvano, celebrating his small successes and feeling grateful that the class can at least provide a predictable environment for him.

Students who are at risk due to mental illness present a special challenge for adult educators. These students also deserve the best experiences and opportunities our system provides.

THE CULTURE OF POVERTY

Many at-risk students come from poverty, as a result of poor choices or generational poverty. Ruby K. Payne in her book, *A Framework for Understanding Poverty,* defines poverty as "the extent to which an individual does without resources" and then lists the resources as financial, emotional, mental, spiritual, physical, support systems, relationships and role models, and knowledge of hidden rules. [10]

Students in poverty present unique challenges because they have limited access to those resources that make going to school easier, such as support systems, mentors, and money. They may have difficulty with childcare, dependable transportation, juggling several low-paying jobs, and other external demands that interfere with their ability to focus on success in school. [11]

A teacher might assume that juggling external demands is easier for incarcerated students because so many of their needs are provided for. This would be a false assumption. Despite their own day-to-day needs being met, students are aware of the struggles their families are going through on the outside, and they feel powerless to help. Their own incarceration often exacerbates the effects of poverty in their family and can lead to further frustration.

Living in poverty may have been what catapulted the student into committing crimes because "crime offers a way in which impoverished people can obtain material goods that they cannot attain through legitimate means." [12] Being aware of one's low socioeconomic status may lead to a perception of having an inferior education, having fewer role models, and having fewer opportunities in the past for academic enrichment. [13]

Students may come to class with a preconceived idea about what is possible in their world and may think that the hopes and opportunities the teacher touts are unrealistic. Often in the students' minds, past experiences are more powerful predictors of their future than the opportunities the teacher presents.

Having students who come from poverty presents challenges to overcome. A teacher must provide background knowledge that most would take for granted and must allow these students to express the reality of their life situation. Teachers must provide scaffolding and make accommodations for how knowledge is gained. These efforts may allow students to see how changing their situation is possible.

A classroom in an inner-city district has a large population of homeless men and women. They bring in their rolling duffle bags, spend long minutes in the bathroom to clean up, and often fail to see how learning multiplication or grammar is important to their lives. Luckily, the teacher of this classroom has a good sense of humor and the ability to build student self-esteem through success in class.

When Irene passed a post-test in punctuation end marks, the teacher made a point of announcing that she was now the class expert and anyone who needed help with end marks should ask her. Irene lit up and then delved diligently into her next lesson, most probably anticipating her next success. For a moment she had forgotten her lack of a stable home and reveled in the celebration of her success.

It is challenging to work with students who feel disenfranchised from the core of society and invite them to become a part of that society. *America's Perfect Storm* points out that engaging the segment of the population that comes from poverty is no longer just a moral obligation; the socioeconomic survival of the nation is at stake. Without this population fully engaged in an education that allows their participation in the nation's economy, jobs will continue to be outsourced, globalization of the economy will make it more difficult for low-skilled workers to find a living wage, and the nation's ability to compete will diminish.[14]

One aim of education is to provide students access to socioeconomic growth and to provide skills for the navigation of available resources they need to survive in our society. Another aim is to teach students appropriate language and behavior or what is considered the "hidden rules" of the middle class without devaluing the values and beliefs they currently hold.

As a presenter at CCARTA Summer Institute, Dr. Igor Koutsenok loves to point out that teachers should praise students when they have good attendance, are punctual, or greet and interact with one another and the teacher in a formal register. Teachers want to praise and reinforce these behaviors because they are most probably not behaviors typical for at-risk students.

CONCLUSION

Each of the traits of at-risk adult students present a unique challenge for teachers. Spending the day with offenders who have a poverty mindset, who have had negative school experiences due to undiagnosed or poorly treated learning disabilities, or who suffer from mental illnesses requires that the teacher be patient, understanding, professional, and hopeful. To be able to see what people may become rather than what they have been is key.

At-risk students present the most difficult challenges for a teacher. Many students present themselves as apathetic, defiant, and/or manipulative. It's important to realize that all of these behaviors are learned self-defense mechanisms to protect the self. Creating a safe environment for the students to explore new ways of seeing themselves in order to be fully engaged academically can be difficult, but these students can be the most rewarding to teach.

Lucky teachers will have unexpected visitors: returning students. These visitors return to share that after having completed the class, they have gone on to continued success. Many will share that they have earned their GED or have gone on to improve their job situation because of their new knowledge and skills. Returning students will often speak briefly to the entire class about being successful. "This is what keeps me going," teachers report.

Teachers who choose to teach at-risk adults work with a population of people that most of society has decided is beyond the reach of rehabilitation. Yet teachers of this population bear witness to the transformative effect education can have.

POINTS TO REMEMBER

- "At risk" is defined as having social, psychological, or economic barriers to attaining socially acceptable standing in society.
- A history of incarceration makes a student at risk.
- Learning disabilities make a student at risk.
- Mental illness makes a student at risk.
- Poverty makes a student at risk.

NOTES

1. Randall Wright, "Going to Teach in Prisons: Culture Shock," *Journal of Correctional Education* 56, no. 1 (March 2005): 22.

2. Edward G. Rozycki, "Identifying the 'At Risk' Student: What Is the Concern?" New Foundations, 2004, http://www.newfoundations.com/EGR/AtRisk.html.

3. Mark Motivans, Bureau of Justice Statistics, US Department of Justice, *Federal Justice Statistics 2009—Statistical Tables*, http://bjs.ojp.usdoj.gov/content/pub/pdf/fjs09st.pdf.

4. Motivans, *Federal Justice Statistics 2009*.

5. "Do I Have LD?" National Center for Learning Disabilities, http://www.ncld.org/adults-learning-disabilities/do-i-have-ld.

6. Motivans, *Federal Justice Statistics 2009*.

7. Mel Levine, *One Mind at a Time* (New York: Simon and Schuster, 2002), 14–15.

8. Erick Eckholm, "Inmates Report Mental Illness at High Levels," *New York Times*, September 7, 2006.

9. Risdon Slate and Wesley W. Johnson, *The Criminalization of Mental Illness: Crisis and Opportunity for the Justice System* (Durham, NC: Carolina Academic Press, 2008), 37–38.

10. Ruby K. Payne, *A Framework for Understanding Poverty* (Highlands, TX: aha! Process Inc., 1996), 7.

11. Payne, *Framework for Understanding Poverty*, 7.

12. Slate and Johnson, *Criminalization of Mental Illness*, 47.

13. Rozycki, "Identifying the 'At Risk' Student."

14. Irwin Kirsh, Henry Braun, Kentaro Yamamoto, and Andrew Sum. 2007. *America's Perfect Storm: Three Forces Changing Our Nation's Future*, 2007, https://www.ets.org/Media/Research/pdf/PICSTORM.pdf.

TWO

Undiagnosed Learning Disabilities and Behavioral Disorders

On the first day of class, John sat in the back and took no notes. He failed to copy down the adjustments to the course syllabus as instructed by the teacher. He watched the board intently, not once turning away to write down any of the key points the teacher wrote there. By the end of the first class session, the teacher wondered why John had even signed up for the class if he wasn't going to participate. What she failed to notice since John was sitting in the back of the class was the recording device he had on his desk and how he took a picture of the board when her back was turned.

In another class across the hall, Mary sat in the front of the class and wrote furiously the entire time the teacher talked, even when other students were talking. She never looked up, never engaged in the class discussions, and never seemed to behave in ways that confirm for most teachers that a student is on-task, is engaged, and is participating. Again, by the end of the session, the teacher wondered why Mary had signed up for the class. He never got the chance to see what Mary had been writing all during class—a transcription of what everyone said for the entire class—because at the end of class she gathered her things and left.

In both of these cases students were fully engaged but in ways that teachers don't immediately recognize as such. Teachers generally gauge student engagement through eye contact, class discussion participation, and taking notes at opportune times during class. Students with learning disabilities, at least those who have devised methods for compensating for their disability, often fail to display these indicators of student engagement because for them to be successful, they must engage in the learning process in a fashion that works for them.

As teachers, it is important to understand the wide range of learning disabilities and how these disabilities may affect student engagement in the classroom. Adult learners with disabilities often come to the class-room with strategies to overcome their disability or with the simple hope that this time the classroom experience may be different, that it may be an environment where they can be successful.

Having a learning disability does not mean that a student is not ca-pable of success. Actually, most students who have a learning disability are of average to above average intelligence. They have the intellectual potential to succeed at school and in careers, but the typical classroom has failed to meet their needs and they have never been taught strategies for overcoming the disability. John and Mary were two of the lucky adult learners because they came to class prepared to use strategies to over-come their disabilities.

Learning disabilities are often referred to as "hidden" disabilities or "non-apparent" disabilities because, though they are caused by a dys-function within the physical body, they are caused by specific dysfunc-tions within the central nervous system—a place in the body not easily seen. The result is a disability not easily identified from the outside.

The central nervous system controls everything we do: our ability to process and think about language, to express ourselves verbally, and to process nonverbal information, including art or music. Hence, the mani-festation of the dysfunction will be different for each person. Some learn-ers will have a disability that interferes with their ability to complete computation while other learners may have a difficult time reading or processing oral language. Not only are disabilities non-apparent, but they are also learner specific.

Cognitive ability or intelligence is our ability to receive, transform, store, and use language and other types of information under a variety of conditions. Most people believe that intelligence is innate or a person is born with a set intelligence quotient (IQ), but others believe that IQ is malleable and is dependent on the environment.

For example, many universities require students to complete the Scho-lastic Aptitude Test (SAT) and submit a score high enough to qualify for university study. Students have a difficult time studying for the SAT because it measures general knowledge and one's ability to use informa-tion in a set condition. It is recognized as a measure of a student's innate intelligence and fails to recognize how intelligence can be context specif-ic.

The reliance on narrow, inflexible measures of intelligence is chang-ing, however. Many companies now hire employees based on their per-formance during a group interview. Those applicants who exhibit the ability to problem-solve, cooperate with others, and communicate clearly are hired because it is believed they can be taught the necessary skills in the right context.

Intelligence is a combination of innate skills and the execution of these skills in context. A student's ability, persistence, and environment all play a role in his success.

Cognitive functioning or thinking involves a set of complete and discrete stages and skills that are needed to connect what a person already knows with the processing and organization of new information. Learning disabilities generally are thought to affect cognitive functions as they may affect one of these discreet stages or skills or may affect several in any number of combinations.

John from the earlier example used strategies to overcome the dyslexia that made it difficult for him to read the board or the handout. He also used strategies to overcome a fine motor skill disability that made it difficult for him to write legibly. He overcame both of these dysfunctions by relying on a recording of the lecture that he could review as many times as needed to understand the information and by taking photos of all written information he would need so he could review them at a slower pace than class allowed.

Learning disabilities are biological, though environmental factors such as schooling and personal supports can make learning more challenging or less challenging. Past school or learning experiences have shaped the adult learner now returning to the classroom. If a person was given support and encouragement within an environment that focused on a student's strengths, likely the adult learner will come to the classroom prepared to request accommodations and to utilize his strengths. On the other hand, if a student was told she was not capable of school work or belittled for her efforts, she may be a reluctant participant in the classroom. Now that the learner is an adult, current living and working experiences, in addition to past experiences, will influence her learning patterns, behavior, and sense of self.

Learners play an active role in the learning process. They use background knowledge about the subject, call on appropriate strategies for both decoding and comprehending new information, and apply the right amount of attention and concentration. These strategies are an essential component of the learning process. Students with or without a learning disability must be actively involved in the learning process for success.

Adult learners must not only actively engage in the intellectual process of learning new materials, but they must also be able to complete the tasks involved in the intellectual work. Many individuals who have learning disabilities have difficulty planning ahead and then evaluating their performance in academic courses or work-related tasks.

Planning involves the ability to determine the outlines of a task and the skills it will require. Planning helps learners generate strategies or know when to ask for outside help. Adult learners may come to class without these skills because in the past their inability to complete the intellectual work prevented them from learning the task-process work involved for success.

As the teacher, being aware of the struggles facing adult learners is key to providing the support and environment in which they will be able to use the strategies that help them be successful. But how does a teacher know when a student needs this type of support?

Though it may be uncomfortable, if a teacher notices a student exhibiting certain learning difficulties, it is a good idea to simply ask. Phrasing the question in a positive light ("When you were in school were you eligible for any special supports?") rather than attempting to figure out the label ("Were you in special education?" or "Are you dyslexic?") allows the student to share the amount of information he or she feels comfortable sharing.

Many students are happy to share their past struggles because they want the teacher to understand their difficulties rather than make assumptions about ability or motivation. There will be students who, because of past teacher insensitivity, will be reluctant to share. In either case, if the teacher asks in a sensitive way, it goes a long way toward creating a safe environment for the learner.

Within the adult student population there is a large number who were not identified with a learning disability for a variety of reasons. Older students will have come through the school system before there were reliable systems for identifying and supporting students with learning disabilities. Other students may not have been identified because of parents who failed to cooperate with the school system because they feared that their child would be labeled as "less than." Other students may have never been identified because of moving schools often. In any case, asking about past school experiences is the best way to learn of past successes and struggles.

Mr. Smith has all students complete a short survey on the first day of class. The survey has questions such as:

1. What are your favorite hobbies?
2. What about school do you like the most?
3. What about school do you struggle with?
4. Why are you here?

This simple survey allows Mr. Smith to immediately begin planning for how to best meet the needs of all students while being sensitive to their strengths and weaknesses.

Many teachers also have students complete surveys, which help them to recognize their learning styles and strengths. A learning style or strength does not necessarily correlate to a specific learning disability but can be used to help students recognize how they best learn.

It is tempting as teachers to want to assess students for learning disabilities. But assessing for learning disabilities—biological, non-apparent dysfunctions—is outside the professional realm of the teacher; it's the purview of medical doctors. Teachers may never know the specific dysfunction of the brain because these assessments are generally costly and time-consuming. But students will know their strengths and weaknesses and teachers can watch for symptoms of each learning disability, not so the teacher can label the student, but so the teacher can modify instruction to best meet the needs of all learners in the classroom.

Teachers who want to be sensitive and prepared for at-risk students must keep in mind that for 80 percent of students with a learning disability, reading is the academic problem.

ATTENTION DEFICIT DISORDER / ATTENTION DEFICIT HYPERACTIVITY DISORDER

Chris is bright, attentive, and a pleasure to have in class. But when his teacher sits down to complete grades, she is shocked to realize that he is failing. Looking through her records, she realizes Chris hasn't turned in most major assignments and the classwork he did turn in was incomplete.

The teacher struggles with giving Chris a grade. She really can't justify passing him without major assignments completed, but she knows he was one of the most articulate and insightful students she has ever had in class. She sits and stares at her final grade-book, at the blank next to Chris's name, the space for his final grade.

Almost every teacher has experienced this type of disconnect between the behaviors a student exhibits in class and the completion of the class assignments. There may be many reasons for this scenario, including ADD or ADHD. Attention deficit disorder (ADD) or attention deficit hyperactivity disorder (ADHD) affects a learner's ability to focus and concentrate on school or work tasks and to make good use of strategies.

The difference between the two disabilities is slight but worth mentioning. Learners with ADD have a difficult time focusing and concentrating. Learners with ADHD not only find focusing and concentrating challenging, but they also have low impulsivity control. ADHD students not only struggle to focus on the delivery of the lesson but struggle to remain seated for the duration of the lesson. Students with ADD or ADHD generally have class work and project grades that lag behind their verbal skills. They may have average or above average intelligence, but they lack strong executive function and good use of the part of their brains that guide decision making.

Because of a struggle with decision-making skills, these students also often have difficulty with self-regulation and difficulty with efficient use of learning strategies. These students appear disorganized and inattentive, and poor academic self-esteem may manifest itself in defensiveness or belligerence when they are confronted.

To avoid confronting students with ADD or ADHD, teachers can be aware of the symptoms. In addition to appearing disorganized and inattentive as just mentioned, these students will also be easily distracted and have quick mood shifts, and they may be impulsive or have low control over their anger.[1] These behaviors are not personality quirks or poor decisions, but a learning disability requiring classroom accommodations.

COMMUNICATION DISORDERS

Sylvia exhibits all the behaviors of a student who is attending to information: tracking the teacher with her eyes, making eye contact, taking notes at appropriate times, and nodding when given instructions. Yet, time after time, Sylvia is unable to complete in-class assignments correctly. Tasks as simple as folding a piece of paper correctly to create a graphic organizer go awry as well as larger assignments such as taking notes in the proper order.

The teacher wonders if there is a language barrier and so one day asks Sylvia if English is her first language. Sylvia is at first surprised to be asked this. "Yes, of course," but then a cloud comes over her features. She has been through this before, confronted with her inability to participate in class successfully.

Communication disorders affect learners in different ways. Sylvia is having a difficult time with oral directions, whereas other students may have difficulty comprehending written directions. Symptoms of communication disorders include speaking problems or an inability to carry on a conversation or express one's thoughts, the inability to remember oral directions, and a delayed response in conversation due to the prolonged time needed to process oral information. There will be a disconnect between what the teacher expects the student to complete when given oral directions and the student's ability to meet those expectations.[2]

VISUAL PROCESSING DISORDER

Being able to see the directions on the board or to manage the written directions on a piece of paper is difficult for students with a visual processing disorder. The problem may be a difficulty in discerning the spaces between the words, distinguishing between letters or numbers that are similar in shape, discerning the written word from the background, copying things from a board or book onto their own paper, or correctly spacing words on the page when writing.

A student with this learning disability may run their words together when writing or fail to observe the margins on the paper when writing.

They may need help finding information on the page or may not be able to track the lines when reading a paragraph and skip lines. If a teacher notices these symptoms, she must refrain from reprimanding the student for what appear to be lazy mistakes and instead provide tools for helping the student to visually track classroom text.[3]

Many of these processing disorders appear similar to other learning disabilities like dyslexia and dysgraphia. They can be very specific to a learner, and a learner may have a combination of these processing disorders. It is important to recognize that the student is not willfully making mistakes in the processing of information.

Students may even refuse to participate in classroom activities such as copying information from the board because, as with John in the example at the beginning of this chapter, they recognize their inability to do these tasks successfully and have strategies for compensating.

DYSLEXIA

It has been reported that between 2 and 8 percent of the population have dyslexia. But, in an adult education classroom with at-risk students, the numbers can be significantly higher. Studies have reported that incarcerated populations have between a 65 percent and 85 percent rate of dyslexia. There is no unanimously accepted definition of this learning disability.

The term *dyslexia* comes from the Greek *dys* meaning "disorder" and *lexicos* meaning "words" and was coined by Rudolf Berlin in 1887. Students with dyslexia have trouble with mastering the competencies required for accurate and automatic word identification. Dyslexia does not correlate with IQ. Though many people will report they have "grown out of" dyslexia, because it is a biological dysfunction, this is not possible and more likely the student has learned to compensate for the disability and find success in spite of it.

Students with dyslexia may say that reading makes them sleepy or that they are slow readers. They will have a difficult time concentrating when reading, will have difficulty explaining what they have just read, and will read in an overly deliberate manner.[4]

DYSGRAPHIA

Writing is considered the most complex form of communication. Writing requires competency in vocabulary, spelling, handwriting, and the formation of sentences and paragraphs. Writers exert effort as they call upon prior knowledge and the conventions of written language to construct a unique product. A student with dysgraphia struggles to complete written assignments because the brain has trouble processing what the learner wants to write.

Adult learners with dysgraphia may avoid writing in class because of their struggles with organizing thoughts and keeping track of what has been written down. When these students do turn in written work, there may be significant errors with syntax and structure and the teacher may recognize a gap between the students' oral skills in class and their writing skills.[5]

DYSCALCULIA

A less well known learning disability is dyscalculia, which affects 6 percent of the population. Students with dyscalculia have problems with recall of math facts. When students are struggling with basic math facts, it is difficult to move on to more abstract ideas. This disability presents itself in a student's inability to retain and retrieve math facts. Students with dyscalculia may transpose numbers (63 and 36), have trouble understanding math symbols (=, –, x, etc.), and have poor math recall skills.[6]

DYSPRAXIA

The final learning disability in the "dys" group is dyspraxia. Dyspraxia affects a student's ability to perform certain physical tasks, for instance jumping rope. Teachers may wonder why they need to be aware of this learning disability if they are not teaching physical education; but as classrooms move more and more to kinesthetic activities, there may be students who struggle with the hands-on activities because of this learning disability.

Students with dyspraxia will fatigue easily, walk with a clumsy gait, and have a tendency to bump into people and objects. When engaged in classroom hands-on activities, they may have difficulty knowing their right hand from their left hand, trouble with using their bodies for demonstration purposes, or trouble performing physical classroom tasks like woodworking or auto mechanics.[7]

AUDITORY PROCESSING DISORDER

Communication disorders include auditory processing disorder or the inability to comprehend oral language. Students who struggle with this disorder will ask for directions to be repeated, be confused about the expectations of assignments if the directions were only given orally, and have a difficult time responding appropriately to oral questions.

To recognize auditory processing disorders, teachers must understand the normal, developmental features of the student's primary language, be able to identify "errors" commonly produced in English that result from the influence of primary language, and determine if the problem with understanding stems from native language interference or an auditory processing disorder.

Because the effect of this disability is an inability to follow oral directions, when a teacher has a student with this disorder, it is imperative that all directions for assignments be written down and that visuals accompany the information when possible.[8]

BEHAVIOR DISORDERS

Many educators choose to teach adults because they believe it will be easier to manage them. But though adult learners are more mature, they may still have behaviors that the teacher must manage.

Adult students have greater life experience than child learners, and this is positive in many ways. But there is also the possibility that these life experiences have resulted in behavioral disorders like post traumatic stress disorder (PTSD) and inappropriate response to common classroom situations.

PTSD affects approximately 8 percent of adults, with the numbers being dramatically higher for those who have served in the armed forces and experienced combat or those who have been victims of crime or other disasters, abuse, or accidents. PTSD can cause students to respond inappropriately in situations that have some similarity to their traumatic event. Students with PTSD are easily startled, may avoid situations that appear to the teacher to be harmless, and may have inexplicably angry outbursts.

When a student is experiencing the symptoms of PTSD, the heightened anxiety makes it difficult to concentrate on metacognition skills and creates poor social perception and judgment. PTSD creates interference with the brain's ability to focus on intellectual tasks because the body goes into "fight or flight" response that causes the blood flow to move toward the body's extremities rather than toward the brain where it is needed. Thinking involves our processing and interpretation of information while metacognition includes our knowledge of ourselves, which affects how we think and learn. If a student is unable to focus on the intellectual tasks before him, this creates further anxiety and may become a vicious cycle.[9]

Other behavioral disorders may be caused by students' antisocial tendencies or other psychological diagnoses that affect their ability to function appropriately in the classroom. For every student, feelings of self-worth, self-esteem, self-efficacy, and self-reliance, as well as drive and motivation to succeed, fall on a continuum between high and low. The degree to which negative experiences can lead to frustration and consequently anger and passivity depends on past experiences and a learner's psychological makeup.

As teachers, knowing a student's psychological disposition is not as important as recognizing that some learners may use self-destructive mechanisms to insulate or protect themselves against failure by withdrawing from or avoiding negative situations and experiences. Some students may use hostility and anger as coping mechanisms, externalizing their anger and disappointment rather than taking personal responsibility for their failure. These students displace or attribute failure to a teacher, a parent, an employer, or an "unfair" test or project.

Learned helplessness—a type of passivity and lack of initiative—is a behavior disorder that helps insulate learners from the trauma of failure. These behaviors serve to shield students from external demands and possible failure. Attribution theory explains that students may believe failure is caused by their low ability. This belief in their low ability has been internalized, giving them no reason to try again. But if students can be taught that failure is related instead to external factors like poor study skills or test-taking skills, they will understand that personal effort can make a difference in their outcomes.[10]

CONCLUSION

Though often adult education teachers go into the profession thinking adult students are more mature and more motivated than children, they often find themselves facing many challenges.

Adults with learning disabilities who are successful are those who are proactive, demonstrate a strong sense of control, have support systems, accept one's disability, and have perseverance and insight.

Teachers can help students with attaining these skills.

POINTS TO REMEMBER

- Teachers don't diagnose learning disabilities, but being aware of symptoms will aid in planning accommodations.
- Most students with learning disabilities have average to above average intelligence.
- Intelligence is malleable and context driven.
- Symptoms of communication disorders include an inability to comprehend written or oral directions.
- Symptoms of visual processing disorders include an inability to read written information or an inability to write legibly.

- Symptoms of dyslexia include reading slowly and an inability to explain what has been read.
- Symptoms of dysgraphia include an inability to write down ideas in a coherent manner.
- Symptoms of dyscalculia include transposing numbers and an inability to comprehend math symbols.
- Symptoms of dyspraxia include being easily fatigued and being clumsy.
- Symptoms of auditory processing problems include an inability to follow oral directions.
- Symptoms of behavior disorders include inappropriate behavioral responses to typical classroom situations.

NOTES

1. Samuel A. Kirk, James J. Gallager, and Nicholaus J. Anastasiow, *Educating Exceptional Children* (New York: Houghton Mifflin, 2003), 266–267.

2. Kirk, Gallager, and Anastasiow, *Educating Exceptional Children*, 323–327.

3. Kirk, Gallager, and Anastasiow, *Educating Exceptional Children*, 420–422.

4. Kirk, Gallager, and Anastasiow, *Educating Exceptional Children*, 220.

5. Kirk, Gallager, and Anastasiow, *Educating Exceptional Children*, 221.

6. Kirk, Gallager, and Anastasiow, *Educating Exceptional Children*, 221–225.

7. Kirk, Gallager, and Anastasiow, *Educating Exceptional Children*, 222–225.

8. Kirk, Gallager, and Anastasiow, *Educating Exceptional Children*, 313.

9. Lisa M. Najavits, *Seeking Safety: A Treatment Manual for PYSD and Substance Abuse* (New York: Guilford Press, 2002), 1–2.

10. Kirk, Gallager, and Anastasiow, *Educating Exceptional Children*, 137.

THREE

Substance Abuse–Induced Brain Dysfunction

Teachers are excited on the first day of class and imagine their students are just as excited about the upcoming term and the potential to gain new knowledge. When a teacher looks out at her classroom full of students, she is filled with optimism about the success of all students enrolled. It is only after days and weeks of working with individual students that specific student needs and challenges begin to present themselves, and the teacher must begin to make accommodations to ensure the possibility of success for all her students.

The assurance that all students have the opportunity to be successful relies on the teacher's ability to meet the challenges of teaching a diverse group of students. One challenge is student use of drugs. A teacher's knowledge of how drugs affect a student's ability to learn will inform her instructional choices.

The National Institute on Drug Abuse reports that as of 2011, approximately 8 percent of Americans use illicit drugs; it estimates that another 8 percent of Americans are using prescription drugs for nonmedical purposes. In addition to these statistics, 12 percent of the population drink alcohol on a regular basis and 35 percent of the population smoke tobacco. These numbers may be higher for the adult classroom filled with students returning to the educational system. Whether the drug of choice is legal or illegal, prescribed or used arbitrarily, all drugs affect the brain and therefore affect learning.

Drugs affect the brain by interfering with the normal process of sending and receiving information. The brain communicates through neurotransmitters. They are involved in all physical, emotional, and cognitive functions, including the reward pathway, or the mesolimbic dopamine system.[1] Neurotransmitters are like signals between cell phones: they are the signals between nerve cells, which are called neurons.

Whenever a person does something, thinks something, or senses something, the neurons in the brain are sending messages to one another about how to interpret and respond to these messages. This communications transmission is affected by drugs. The body has a blood-brain barrier that keeps most harmful substances out of the brain, like cell towers that keep interference out of cell transmissions. Unfortunately, once drugs are in the bloodstream, they pass easily through this barrier and affect the brain. Drugs scramble the messages between nerves by either blocking the messages or intensifying the messages.

Drugs are either stimulants or depressants to a learner's body. They either stimulate the messages, making them seem more urgent or excitable than they actually are, or depress the messages, making them seem more relaxed and non-urgent than they actually are. In either case, a person affected by drugs does not think clearly.

An important part of learning is the ability to regulate the executive functions of the brain carried out by the frontal lobe. These functions include judgment, decision making, and controlling impulses. Drugs distort the brain's ability to complete these functions. Students under the influence of drugs, whether they are currently "high" or "hung-over," will have difficulty with good judgment, with understanding what is and is not important, as well as with learning new material. They will struggle with following directions and remembering new information.

Most students will not be drug dependent, but even casual use affects a person's ability to learn new information, retrieve past information, and store new information into long-term memory. There are immediate effects of drug use on learning and long-term effects.

SHORT-TERM EFFECTS OF CHEMICAL ABUSE

Just about everyone has awakened feeling like her brain isn't in gear and getting it in gear requires some stimulation, whether it's a cup of coffee, a morning cigarette, or maybe just some deep stretching. And we all have times when we can't focus because we have too much on our minds. Worrying about a loved one's health, distracted by plans for later in the week, or trying to keep up with a busy schedule can all interfere with a person's ability to concentrate.

There are natural ebbs and flows of the ability of the brain to focus. Sometimes our brain is too stimulated and sometimes not stimulated enough. Imagine going through the day without your morning cup of coffee if you are a heavy coffee drinker, or if you aren't a coffee drinker how excitable you are when you do drink coffee. Caffeine is a mild stimulant and affects the brain much the same way illicit or prescription drugs do, though on a very low level. Students who use drugs have these same effects but on more extreme levels. They may come to class with their brain in a drug-induced fog or a drug-induced frenzy.

Students who use drugs, whether casually or habitually, may be trying to pay attention when their neurotransmitters either are resting from being overstimulated the night before or are on high alert because of rebounding from being depressed unnaturally the night before.

The short-term effects of using drugs on the brain are many. First there will be an unnatural level of dopamine. Dopamine regulates energy and pleasure and can either help students to feel energetic or prevent them from this feeling. Another effect is an unnatural level of epinephrine or norepinephrine, which regulate alertness. A student's ability to pay attention will be affected by the levels of these chemicals in the brain.[2]

Next, drugs affect the level of serotonin in the brain, which regulates mood. Research has shown that students who are happy are more receptive to learning whereas students who are unhappy or frightened have difficulties paying attention. Drugs can also alter the levels of acetylcholine in the brain, which regulates memory. A low level of acetylcholine in the brain will make it difficult for students to remember much of what happens in class. Finally, drugs affect the level of GABA in the brain, which regulates judgment and impulsivity,[3] perhaps creating classroom management challenges for the teacher.

In any case, learners who are using drugs are not in an optimal state for learning. Unfortunately, if their drug use is prolonged, these effects are multiplied and worsened.

LONG-TERM EFFECTS OF CHEMICAL ABUSE

There is a large population of adult students who are returning to the classroom for a second chance. After years of drug abuse, they are ready to integrate into society in a healthy way and see education as a way to get there. As the teacher of these students, it is helpful to understand what these learners are battling to be successful in the classroom.

The long-term effect of chemical abuse is dependence on the drug of choice. If a student is currently dependent on a drug, he will be unable to function in class when his body is in need of the drug. It's like trying to pay attention when you're hungry; anyone who has fasted for even a day can remember how every moment is consumed with the thought of food and eating. Likewise, a drug-dependent learner is unable to focus on learning when drug deprived.

In addition to the distraction of cravings, drug-dependent students also battle the effects of long-term use on the brain and body. A drug-dependent student is likely to have impaired functioning in the storage and retrieval of memories and the moderation of the executive functions of the brain, including judgment and decision making. They may have liver problems or breathing problems. If a student is dealing with a health issue, this may interfere with his ability to concentrate on his studies, to attend class, or to complete assignments.

The chronic use of alcohol affects a learner in many ways as well. Alcohol abuse damages the liver, the pancreas, and the central nervous system, and it causes a general wearing down of systems that can result in psychological and psychiatric problems. Behavior effects include reduced judgment and reaction time, impaired concentration and coordination, and slowed reflexes. These behavior effects interfere with learning.[4]

Health problems associated with long-term tobacco use include lung cancer, emphysema, circulatory problems, heart problems, and strokes. Smoking tobacco reduces the blood's ability to carry oxygen to body systems, including the brain. If the brain is not getting enough oxygen, it is unable to function at optimal levels. Research has linked cigarette smoking to cognitive decline, reduced memory, and brain shrinkage.[5]

Though many smokers will claim they smoke to relieve stress, research shows that smokers have higher levels of stress than nonsmokers, and any reports of being more alert diminish once the body has built a tolerance to nicotine. Unfortunately, because the body builds tolerance for nicotine, if a person quits smoking, her ability to concentrate and think clearly will diminish until the body is able to fully recover.

The effects of cocaine or amphetamines (meth) include weight loss, sores on the skin, bone loss (often evident in the loss of teeth), and poor judgment. Both of these drugs are stimulants, which users will report help them to think clearly and get more done. Unfortunately, stimulants also reduce concentration and increase excitability.[6]

Another effect of long-term drug use is the contraction of chronic illnesses such as tuberculosis. A student with a chronic illness will often have difficulty concentrating on academic challenges or may suffer symptoms of the illnesses that interfere with attendance. Drug use often is accompanied by a lack of attention to hygiene and health precautions, which may lead users to continue to suffer from illnesses contracted during their drug use, putting their overall health in jeopardy for the rest of their lives.

Finally, withdrawal from some drugs can prompt symptoms that resemble mental illness. The symptoms' severity, frequency, and duration depend on the drug of use and the amount of use.

These are the long-term health effects of prolonged abuse of drugs. A teacher may have students who have been sober for many years and yet continue to struggle with the long-term health effects of their past use. Even after sobriety, previous long-term drug use can continue to affect students. Generally the body takes twenty-eight days to clear chemicals from the major body systems. Unfortunately, the brain takes years to rebalance itself after prolonged drug use. This rebalancing of the brains is called post acute withdrawal syndrome and has significant implications for learners.

POST ACUTE WITHDRAWAL SYNDROME

Sally routinely pulled her sweatshirt sleeves well past her wrists in an attempt to hide her tattoos. She was in her second semester at the local community college and working hard to rebuild her life after ten years "in the game," as she called it. Though she had been sober for eight months, she told her teacher she was having a difficult time remembering things and concentrating in class. She further explained that because of her recovery classes she knew these problems were to be expected in early sobriety, but they were no less frustrating.

Post acute withdrawal syndrome (PAWS) is a set of persistent impairments that occur after a person has stopped using drugs, has detoxed from drugs, and is working toward living a sober lifestyle. PAWS is a result of the brain's neurotransmitters regaining balance after being artificially stimulated. The syndrome can last from a year to several decades. These impairments affect everyday life, including causing general cognitive deficiencies.[7]

Cognitive symptoms of PAWS include impaired concentration, the inability to think clearly, and memory problems. Though a student will report having been sober for years, his brain may still be recovering and his ability to learn may be affected.

Other symptoms of PAWS that affect a learner's ability to be successful in the classroom include impaired interpersonal skills, lack of initiative, emotional overreactions or numbness, sleep disturbances, and stress sensitivity. If a student is feeling challenged by the materials presented in class and therefore is feeling stressed, her ability to deal with that stress may be impaired.[8]

As a teacher, it is important to understand that there are triggers for PAWS symptoms. These include stressful or frustrating situations, attempts at multitasking, feelings of anxiety, fearfulness or anger, social conflicts, unrealistic expectations of the self, and feelings of being overwhelmed with tasks to complete.

HOW CHEMICAL ABUSE AFFECTS LEARNING

Whether students are using drugs casually, are dependent on drugs, or are recovering from drug use, their ability to learn is affected. Think about a reluctant learner and how stress interferes with his ability to concentrate; now multiply that exponentially because of the brain's dysfunction from drug use. Think about an older learner and her struggles with remembering key concepts; now multiply that exponentially because of the brain's dysfunction from drug use. It is critical for teachers to remember that all the natural barriers to learning are exacerbated by a student's drug use.

Students who are facing these difficulties in the classroom should be reminded to take deep breaths. Getting more oxygen to the brain helps to balance the nerves in a natural way and helps the brain to become more relaxed and able to focus. It's a natural way to nudge the brain into behaving in ways that are conducive to learning goals.

CONCLUSION

According to the National Institute on Drug Abuse, as many as 28 percent of students in any classroom are ingesting drugs that change the chemicals in their brains and affect their ability to learn. Teachers who are aware of these challenges are better equipped to offer success to all students.

POINTS TO REMEMBER

- All drugs change the brain's ability to receive and retrieve information.
- Short-term effects of drug use include changes in mood, memory, and judgment.
- Long-term effects of drug use include changes in memory functions, the ability to concentrate, and psychological stability.
- Post acute withdrawal syndrome effects include a lack of initiative, sleep disturbances, and stress sensitivity.
- Drug-induced brain dysfunction creates learner challenges.

NOTES

1. Carlton Erickson, *Alcohol, Drugs and the Brain* (Georgetown, TX: FMS Productions, 2011), DVD.
2. Erickson, *Alcohol, Drugs and the Brain.*
3. Erickson, *Alcohol, Drugs and the Brain.*
4. John Keppler, *Alcohol and Drugs, Body and Mind: The Medical Consequences* (Georgetown, TX: FMS Productions, 2011), DVD.
5. Keppler, *Alcohol and Drugs, Body and Mind.*
6. Keppler, *Alcohol and Drugs, Body and Mind.*
7. Darryl S. Inaba, William E. Cohen, Elizabeth von Radics, and Ellen K. Cholewa, *Uppers, Downers, All Arounders: Physical and Mental Effects of Psychoactive Drugs* (Medford, OR: CNS Productions, 2011), 71–72.
8. Inaba et al., *Uppers, Downers,* 71–72.

FOUR

Chronic Criminogenic Behaviors

Carl comes to class at least fifteen minutes late when he shows up at all. He is very apologetic and promises it won't happen again, but then it does. The teacher decides to talk to Carl about his tardiness and while planning for the "discussion" observes his in-class behavior a bit more closely than usual. What she witnesses worries her.

She notices that Carl does not participate in the pair-share or any group discussions. Instead he slouches in his chair and stares out the window or pulls out his phone and appears to be texting with the phone in his lap. She also notices that Carl's eyes are suspiciously bloodshot, which she hopes is caused by working odd hours to fit school into a busy schedule.

At break the teacher asks Carl to stay after. Once all the other students have left, the teacher begins.

"I've noticed that you are coming to class late on a regular basis. Is there something I can help you with?"

"No, I just come late so I can skip the boring stuff at the beginning," Carl answers earnestly.

"I review the previous lesson at the beginning to prepare for the day's lesson so I feel it is important that you are here for that."

"That's okay. I don't need review," Carl answers again without guile.

The teacher decides to take a different tack. "Well, it is also disruptive to the other students when you come in late."

"Who's complaining?" Carl furrows his brow and frowns.

"That's not the point—"

"Are you having a bad day or what?" Carl smiles warmly. When the teacher shakes her head, Carl drops his smile and adds, "You can't drop me just because I'm not on your schedule."

The teacher feels like she and Carl are having two different conversations. It has become apparent to her that Carl's sense of following the classroom expectations and her expectations are quite different.

American public education was founded as a path to creating a homogenous culture, a way to make our democracy work. Over 150 years later, it is one of the few institutions open to anyone who wants an education. Schools are a place to learn valuable skills for the workplace, but they are also places where the values of our culture are shared.

Values are at the heart of any culture, and teachers, through their actions, words, and expectations for students, bring a set of values to the classroom. Though teachers may believe they are being culture neutral, they are bringing cultural values to the classroom, and so are the students. To deal with this fact, they must take what is called a "transactional, situational approach." This approach recognizes that each student has "unique needs, characteristics, and strengths."[1] It encourages teachers to be respectful of the culture a student brings to the classroom while at the same time modeling for the student the values of the educational institution — those that students will need to succeed in the outside world.

Unfortunately, many teachers mistakenly overgeneralize characteristics of certain cultures to all students perceived as coming from that culture. A better approach is to approach each student as a unique individual and to build an understanding of a student's culture and values through asking questions about the student's expectations, values, and motivation.

The teacher in the previous example believed that Carl was late because of an overburdened schedule, something she is familiar with as a single parent who juggles childcare, working, and other obligations. But, in her interaction with Carl, she realized that he is tardy because he fails to value what is happening in the class and the idea of punctuality.

Many students wish to have their culture respected while also desiring to move into the dominant culture. To do this, students have to go through the process of "acculturation" — learning to integrate into their own life behavior norms that are more in line with the pervasive American norms of behavior — norms that are critical to success in the marketplace.[2] There are many factors that prevent acculturation: diverse backgrounds, educational level, place of residence, feelings of discomfort with fitting into the new culture, and so on.

Acculturation can be especially difficult for students who have a criminal record. A criminal record is not necessarily an indication that the student has come from and embraces a culture that is counter to the prevailing culture and values. But often these students have been on the fringes of society for their entire lives and have grown comfortable with the values of this alternative culture. To identify students with chronic criminogenic behaviors a teacher can listen for negative attitudes toward the law, authority figures, conventional institutions, conventional values, conventional rules, conventional procedures, and one's ability to achieve through conventional means.

These students may also exhibit a lack of empathy toward others and display criminogenic qualities. Criminogenic qualities are those that are commonly thought to contribute to criminal behavior. They include having an antisocial personality, antisocial attitudes and values, antisocial associates, family dysfunction, poor self-control, poor problem-solving skills, and what is known as "criminal thinking."

ANTISOCIAL PERSONALITY

When observing Carl, the teacher noticed that Carl did not participate in the pair-share or group work and he also ignored requests from other students to engage. Questions like "Carl, what do you think?" were met with icy glares or outright aggressive responses such as "None of your business. Just do your work and don't worry about me." The teacher had seen this type of behavior in the past and attributed it to student feelings of discomfort with his or her peers and a fear of exposing an inability to contribute to the group in a meaningful way. This is correct on many levels.

The official diagnosis for antisocial personality is the "pervasive pattern of disregard for and violation of the rights of others."[3] Students with this disorder often have below average verbal intelligence and weak problem-solving skills, which can lead to reluctance to working in groups.

Another barrier to working in groups for these students is they have weak socialization skills and may be impulsive with a lack of coping skills or self-regulation skills. On top of this, they most likely find the classroom boring because they tend to be adventurous and pleasure seeking. Finally, their egocentrism and restless aggressiveness make it difficult to function appropriately in the traditional classroom.

This definition is broad and the predispositions of these students may manifest in a classroom in many different ways, but they will become most prevalent when students are asked to work in groups or when students are expressing their values during class discussion.

ANTISOCIAL ATTITUDES AND VALUES

When the teacher tried to discuss his lack of punctuality, Carl made it clear that he did not value being on time and didn't care about his teacher's opinion of him. This is an example of an antisocial attitude, and it can manifest in several ways.

Antisocial students may be angry when they are confronted with a failure to meet the expectations of the classroom or to act in a pro-social manner. They may feel backed into a corner or disrespected, which triggers rage or defiance. Antisocial students may also have a criminal identity, a self-concept that is based in rejection of the social norms and "square" behavior of the larger society. This self-identity may manifest in statements like "regular jobs are for chumps," "I want fast money," or "I don't need to know this because I have connections."[4]

Teachers faced with these attitudes may wonder why the student is attending class at all. If asked, many students will tell the teacher they are being forced to attend by someone with authority over them, whether that someone is a probation officer, parole agent, family member, or the courts. The challenge for teachers confronted with such attitudes is to continue to offer the student a valuable experience.

ANTISOCIAL ASSOCIATES

Another reason that Carl fails to interact with his classmates is because none of them look like, act like, or respond to him like his friends. He feels like a red ball in a room full of blue blocks. Carl is used to hanging out with people like him, not people who are attending school.

Students with criminogenic behaviors will socialize with others who hold their same values. Even if the student is trying to change his life, he will leave the classroom to return to an environment that supports criminogenic values. This often means there is no support system for the student to encourage him to, for example, complete homework assignments, and it results in isolation from the students in class who hold values accepted by the larger society. Instead of leaving the classroom and working with other students in the library or at the student union, this student will leave the classroom to be surrounded by people who will misunderstand and even belittle the student's efforts at completing school.

FAMILY DYSFUNCTION

Most at-risk students come from homes where there was a high level of dysfunction, creating educational obstacles to overcome for the rest of their lives. As children these students had poor parental supervision and discipline practices if not outright neglect and abuse. Without the proper guidance and support as children, these students have grown into adults who lack the discipline and esteem needed to be successful at school.

One student shared that she missed school every Monday growing up because her mom took her with her to work on Mondays. Her mom was a housekeeper and on Mondays she cleaned a large house and needed help. The student is convinced her mom just wanted company. Now, as an adult, this woman has a difficult time with attendance, not to mention completing schoolwork, since her mom never even asked about home-work let alone made sure she completed it. Her childhood habits hinder her progress now as an adult learner.

Growing up with a low level of caring, affection, and cohesiveness within the family, these students will struggle when asked to work with others in the class and with trusting the instructor to have their best interest at heart.[5] Carl has learned to be suspicious of anyone in authority since he was never able to depend on his own parents.

The hardest family dysfunction to overcome may be a family history of crime. When a child grows up with a parent or close relatives who have been incarcerated, a criminogenic lifestyle becomes "normal." It is important to understand that going to school and functioning in a pro-social situation feel very uncomfortable for these at-risk students.

POOR SELF-CONTROL

Charles wanted to know his grade on a major project. The teacher ex-plained that she hadn't graded it yet. Charles was impatient and insisted that she grade it now.

"It's not here. I took it home to grade," the teacher explained.

"Well, it better be graded by next class!" he insisted.

Charles's reaction to his disappointment over his grade illustrates one of the most common difficulties for students with criminogenic behav-iors: impulse control. And yet such self-control is one of the most critical traits for successful learning. This was displayed in Stanford University's famous marshmallow test: In 1972 researchers at Stanford placed chil-dren in a room with a marshmallow (or some other treat that appealed to them) in front of each one. They were told that they could eat the treat any time, but if they waited fifteen minutes before eating it, they could get a second treat. In follow-up studies over the years, researchers found that the children who waited for the treat, and thus exhibited greater self-control, were much likelier to do well in school and on SAT exams. The process of delaying immediate pleasure in favor of future rewards turned out to be key for learning.

Many at-risk students are predisposed to low self-control. They may have been raised in an environment where no one exhibited self-control and been socialized into a culture that did not reward delayed gratifica-tion. Students with poor self-control will have a difficult time waiting their turn in class discussions or waiting for feedback on assignments. They may react with anger to delays or obstructions. Teachers can help these students by putting consistent structure and procedures in place. Clear expectations regarding procedures will help them behave as ex-pected in the classroom. Teachers should also make it clear that anger is always inappropriate in the school setting.

POOR PROBLEM SOLVING

Another feature of criminogenic behavior is a lack of problem-solving skills.

When Carl was confronted with his lack of punctuality, the teacher offered to help Carl with whatever challenges he was facing that contributed to his lateness. Carl didn't see his lateness as a problem, but if he had, chances are he would have told the teacher that it couldn't be helped. Students who are late will often explain that the bus they take or the ride they catch always drops them off at "that time"; and when asked if they might make other arrangements, these students are either unable or unwilling to think of possible solutions to the problem.[6]

At-risk students often have poor problem-solving skills. They accept situations as they are and don't feel the need—or think they have the ability—to change them. When faced with obstacles to success, they fall into a "criminal thinking" pattern of blaming: they feel they are victims of their circumstances and are powerless to change them.[7]

This can be frustrating for a teacher. When a teacher confronts them with a problem, instead of trying to find a solution, at-risk students may use mollification or try to calm the teacher down. They may use phrases like "you are overreacting," "it's not as bad you're making it," or "you must be having a bad day; let me help you." This can feel very patronizing to a teacher, but it's important to not take it personally and instead be firm: make clear to the student why their behavior is problematic and re-state that expectations must be met.[8]

CRIMINAL THINKING

Criminal thinking is a mindset that arises from immersion in a criminogenic environment and holds attitudes and values that are opposed to those of the mainstream culture. In particular, criminal thinking is characterized by shortcuts and by a lack of connection between the student's effort and their eventual success. Earlier we discussed the criminal thinking attitude of blaming and feeling that circumstances are out of the student's control. Other types of criminal thinking demonstrate a similar disconnect between the student's effort and their success in learning.

One such type of criminal thinking involves feelings of entitlement. Many students will feel that because they have been incarcerated, the government owes them—either because of the time they lost while incarcerated or because they are no longer perpetuating crimes. When a teacher is trying to help these students with planning for success and addressing obstacles to success, they may not heed suggestions for improvement or warnings about potential failure. During class, they may exhibit cognitive indolence or mental laziness and feel that they have done their part simply by showing up. They may also fail to make an effort because they have never been successful in the classroom before and don't feel that they can meet with success, so they decide not to try.

Another type of criminal thinking involves discontinuity or never following through on plans.[9] Many students, without the proper support, most likely will not complete the class or not complete major assignments in order to pass the class. Their background has not prepared them to be aware of deadlines or be conscientious about details. Teacher support can help with this.

Ironically, another common mindset for at-risk students is super optimism. Some students may feel that because they are trying to "live right," everything will (and should) come easy to them.[10] This is yet another type of disconnect between effort and result.

It is important to remember that criminal behaviors often co-occur with substance abuse. Hence, not only are there criminal thinking patterns interfering with a student's success in the class, but these students are most likely suffering from the brain dysfunction of substance abuse.

Finally, one odd manifestation of criminal thinking is that a student may attempt to "help" the teacher with class control. This may be an attempt to assert power in the classroom on the student's part or a lack of faith in authority structures. Without engaging in a power struggle, teachers must exert their authority and reassure students that their help is not needed for classroom management.

CONCLUSION

Though a criminal record does not necessarily predict a student's behaviors in class, teachers who are aware of criminogenic behaviors will be better equipped to manage the behaviors and attitudes that might interfere with student success.

POINTS TO REMEMBER

- Criminogenic behavior is most easily identified by negative attitudes to authority or conventional societal norms.
- Antisocial personality behaviors include weak socialization skills and a lack of coping skills.
- Antisocial attitudes and values manifest in behaviors such as rejecting social norms.
- Growing up with a low level of family cohesiveness results in students who are suspicious of authority figures.
- Students with poor self-control may have hostile outbursts in the classroom.

- Students with poor problem-solving skills fail to overcome minor setbacks.
- Criminal thinking displays a disconnect between student effort and educational success.

NOTES

1. Celeste Roseberry-McKibbin, *Multicultural Students with Special Language Needs: Practical Assessment and Intervention* (Oceanside, CA: Academic Communication Associates, 2002), 10.

2. Roseberry-McKibbin, *Multicultural Students with Special Language Needs*, 10.

3. Michael B. First, Allen Frances, and Harold Alan Pincus, *DSM-IV-TR Handbook of Differential Diagnosis* (Arlington, VA: American Psychiatric Publishers, 2002).

4. Stanton Samenow, *Inside the Criminal Mind* (New York: Crown, 2004), 31.

5. Samenow, *Inside the Criminal Mind*, 29.

6. Samenow, *Inside the Criminal Mind*, 57.

7. Samenow, *Inside the Criminal Mind*, 229.

8. Samenow, *Inside the Criminal Mind*, 176.

9. Samenow, *Inside the Criminal Mind*, 62.

10. Samenow, *Inside the Criminal Mind*, 228.

FIVE

The Adult Brain

Once upon a time science believed that the brain developed until a certain age, then its capacity began to diminish. Included in this theory was the belief that if a portion of the brain was damaged, the injury was permanent. A teacher looking out at a classroom of older adults may have been dismayed at the potential of students with such deficits. Luckily, today science has turned this theory on its head.

Research conducted in the last decade using brain imaging has proven not only that the brain has plasticity, or the ability to create new routes to learn new information and recover previously learned knowledge, but that the brain is like a muscle. It stays healthy and functioning when "exercised." And yet, like muscles, there are some functions of the brain that diminish as the brain ages.[1]

Brain capacity continues to grow until a person is in his or her late twenties. Once the brain is done growing, it begins and then continues the process of pruning or cutting pathways to learned information it does not need. To understand development of the brain and how pruning works, a review of how the brain functions will help.

The brain is divided into several lobes. The frontal lobes found behind a person's forehead are responsible for problem solving, judgment, and motor function. The parietal lobes found under the top of the skull manage sensation, handwriting, and body position. The temporal lobes found under the skull where the ears are control memory and hearing. Finally, the occipital lobes found behind the base of the skull contain the brain's visual processing system.

The brain also has many areas that work together. The cerebral cortex is the outermost layer of brain cells; this is the famous "gray matter" that is responsible for initiating thought and controlling voluntary movements. The brain stem is between the spinal cord and the rest of the brain and controls basic functions such as breathing and sleep. The cerebellum is at the back under the occipital lobes and controls coordination and balance. The basal ganglia found deep within the brain coordinates messages between the other areas of the brain.

The areas that are most important to the process of learning include the cerebellum, the thalamus, the hippocampus, and the middle brain. The cerebellum makes predictions based on past performance and the internal conditions necessary in other regions of the brain to perform. In other words, it predicts if the learner will be able to complete any given task. The thalamus aids a learner's ability to pay attention. The hippocampus is responsible for making meaning out of stored memories and converting information from working memory to long-term memory. Finally, the middle brain acts as an emotional clearing house and emotions are important to learning.

Each person also has what is called brain dominance. The left brain generally controls writing, reading, and speaking, which all require the brain to think in a linear sequence. Left-brain dominant thinkers are prone to see the world as "part to the whole" and to be detail oriented.

The right brain controls a person's awareness of feelings, allows for options or choices to be explored, helps with the processing of original information, and is where images are visualized and imagination is nurtured. Right-brain dominant thinkers tend to see the world as "whole to parts" and be big picture thinkers.

Generally, students who are right-handed tend to be left-brain dominant and students who are left-handed tend to be right-brain dominant. Much like hand dominance, brain dominance can depend on the situation, the task being completed, and training. A person who has been right-handed his whole life but then loses the use of this hand can train himself to use his left hand proficiently for all tasks. Likewise, a student who has a predisposition for left-brain thinking can train herself to use the right brain functions proficiently.

Finally, a person's nutritional habits, sleep habits, and exercise habits all have an effect on the brain's health.

THE EFFECTS OF AGING ON THE BRAIN

Many people fear a loss of mental capacity as they age. In the classroom, an older student may feel intimidated by the younger students because of a perceived difference in the brain ability. Teachers know that though younger students may have advantages because of their familiarity with technology, students of all ages can learn the material presented in a classroom.

As mentioned earlier, the conventional wisdom had been that as a person starts to age, the brain ages too. And while some adults do feel effects of aging, many are able to maintain their mental capacities. As a healthy brain ages, it goes through normal physical changes with the most noticeable change in short-term memory. Everyone has wondered "Where did I leave my keys?" but the older brain also wonders "Why did I come in this room?"

While the aging brain struggles with short-term memory, long-term memory and recall decline only slightly. The ability to problem solve seems to decline only if the brain has been lazy or not stimulated. When adults engage in challenging mental stimulation, the brain's connections between neurons increase, which results in greater recall of stored memories.[2] Many doctors now recommend that older adults engage in challenging intellectual activities every day to keep the brain working.

Likewise, keeping stress levels under control promotes greater memory and recall. Unfortunately, adults tend to become stressed when learning new information, especially if they are comparing themselves to younger classmates. Stress results in interference in optimal brain functioning. Not only does a proper amount of sleep help with reducing stress, it also is an essential component for learning or forming new memories.

So, though the adult brain does go through some normal changes, its plasticity means that its cognitive decline is negligible. And while auditory and visual memory may decline as a student ages, kinesthetic memory remains intact and relatively strong throughout one's lifetime.

ADULT EXPERIENCES AND THE BRAIN

When Martha entered the computer lab, she stared at the screen while all the other students logged on. She waited until the teacher came around to help her individually, at which time she admitted that she had never really used a computer before and had been laid off her last job because she was computer illiterate. The teacher tried to convince Martha that using a computer was easy. Every time Martha made a mistake she mumbled, "This is not easy."

When teaching children, educators worry about managing student experiences to create a positive environment. Teaching adults, on the other hand, may mean not only managing immediate classroom experiences but also past experiences adults bring with them to the classroom. For the at-risk learner, these experiences, especially those associated with school, are often negative.

Not only do adults bring past classroom and school experiences with them, but they live multidimensional lives and often come to class with stress from family, work, and past trauma. The emotional residue of these experiences can affect the learner's current experience of the classroom.

Just like any learner, adult learners' brains react to classroom situations in ways that can either enhance learning or become a barrier to learning.[3] Because the primal brain, or the brain stem, controls all involuntary reactions and often overrides the voluntary portion of the brain, emotional memories receive greater attention, become elaborately arranged, and can be activated even when the event is in the past. This emotional energy can be triggered by both positive and negative memories, with negative memories having more strength. For example, many students can recall in great detail those teachers they loved, but with greater detail those teachers they hated.

If a learner is experiencing positive emotions, the brain becomes stimulated, making it easier to focus attention, memory, and higher-level thinking skills on learning. At-risk learners have few past positive experiences associated with school and so lack the positive brain stimulation that would help them focus on learning. If students share their negative experiences with the teacher, the teacher has the opportunity to acknowledge their experiences but also open up the possibility for new positive experiences in the present. A teacher can reassure students with comments like "That was a long time ago; you have changed as a person with new experiences and knowledge. Plus your brain continued to develop until now. I bet you can accomplish this now since you are more mature and experienced." This will help students to be open to a positive, successful current classroom experience.

Brain function can also be impaired when a learner feels threatened within the classroom. Because of past experiences, the learner's brain may perceive classroom learning as a dangerous situation, and the self-preservation rather than the processing part of the brain will be engaged. This triggers a survival response, causing all the body's blood flow to be directed to the body's extremities in preparation for fight or flight. The brain shifts into primal mode, basically cutting off the brain's ability to reason in lieu of its need to preserve itself.

An effective classroom will be filled with challenging educational opportunities. Stretching students' skills and challenging them is the educator's job. But it is crucial to provide a balance between learning and safety, between feelings of challenge and positive emotions. Once the learner registers the threat as non-life-threatening, rational thought processes can take over, and a more appropriate response can be generated. If the learner continues to perceive the environment, instructor, or content to be personally threatening, the learner may not be able to shift out of threat mode and into higher cognitive functions.[4] Hence, there is a need for balance.

Ultimately, the learner should be in the state called "flow." This is the highest level of learning brought about by active engagement in a challenging and stimulating learning environment or experience. Once the learner enters the flow state, intrinsic motivation and commitment to learning predominates. The learner finds the subject to be personally meaningful and therefore becomes personally committed to learning.[5]

REFLECTION AND THE ADULT BRAIN

When Trude learned in her college anatomy class that the jaw was the strongest bone in the face, she began to think about all the times she had opened packages with her teeth, or the times she had seen people hanging from a rope by clasping their teeth on it. She had been told over and over not to open things with her teeth, yet the urge was often irresistible and now she knew why. After reflection she understood; teeth are not the strongest bones in the face, but the jaw bone is.

Reflection is a thinking process by which learners think about new information and decide how it fits into what they already know and what goals they have for learning the information. Students use reflection when the information learned is rather complicated or unstructured and requires more processing or understanding. Because adults bring so much life experience with them and because their brains work at a more modest pace, it is important to pace the classroom instruction to meet their need for reflective time.

No one forces adults to go to school, and yet over one million adults return to school each year to seek more education, further their job skills, or learn skills for personal reasons. Because returning to school by choice, most adult learners are self-directed and autonomous. The new knowledge they are hoping to gain will help to improve their productivity and will increase their quality of living, but only if it is integrated into their existing knowledge and experiences.

All learners, but adults especially, need to make sense out of the world, to find meaning in their lives, and to be effective at those aspects of life they most highly value. When adult learners sign up for a class, they expect one or all of these desires to be met. When new information is inconsistent with their personal experiences and values, the information may be quickly forgotten.

Allowing time for students to reflect on the new information and how it fits with experience and prior knowledge permits students to further process the information until it makes sense.[6] For example, class discussions allow for the teacher to elicit feedback and increase student involvement, which makes learning meaningful.

Finally, for adult learners who, as mentioned earlier in the chapter, have brains that are still very strong in kinesthetic memory, combining movement with mental and sensory rehearsal of new learning concepts makes those concepts more likely to be retained automatically.

TWO BRAINS ARE BETTER THAN ONE, MORE BRAINS IS BEST

Often the students in an adult education classroom will feel they have more in common with each other than with the teacher. And many times, they will learn a great deal from each other when given the chance.

Adult learners have a variety of experiences. In Frederick's classroom when he was teaching how to write a summary, many students expressed the idea that they would never need this skill in the workplace. Charles, an older student, chimed in and explained that in his old job as a security guard, he wrote summaries of incidents all the time. A student challenged Charles, stating, "I don't plan on being a security guard." To which Charles replied, "Son, you will have to write summaries in any job if you want to be promoted."

Generally adults want to share their experiences. Sharing these experiences with other students and the teacher validates their prior knowledge. Being able to interact with one another makes a great environment for group collaboration and for sharing of real-world knowledge.

CONCLUSION

The adult brain stays healthy when students exercise their brains through learning and take care of their health. Teaching to the adult brain means organizing instruction to fit their prior knowledge, their desire to interact with others, and their willingness to share their knowledge.

POINTS TO REMEMBER

- The adult brain stays healthy and functioning when exercised.
- The aging brain struggles with short-term memory.
- Keeping stress levels low helps the adult brain function optimally.
- Negative past experiences can influence an adult student's current experience of the classroom.
- The state of "flow" is the best learning situation.
- Students use reflection to fit new information and skills into existing knowledge.
- Students learn from other students with diverse experiences.

NOTES

1. Laurie Materna, *Jump Start the Adult Learner: How to Engage and Motivate Adults Using Brain-Compatible Strategies* (Thousand Oaks, CA: Corwin Press, 2007), 39–41.
2. Materna, *Jump Start the Adult Learner*, 93–94.
3. Materna, *Jump Start the Adult Learner*, 7.
4. Materna, *Jump Start the Adult Learner*, 4–5.

5. Materna, *Jump Start the Adult Learner,* 19.
6. Materna, *Jump Start the Adult Learner,* 19.

SIX

Managing the At-Risk Adult Learner

At the annual conference of training for teachers and correctional agents, there is a talent show. One of the staples of this talent show is the skit depicting the typical classroom. Teachers argue over who is going to have to play "the teacher" because everyone wants to act as "the student."

The skit goes like this—teacher stands at the front of the staged classroom and greets students as they file into the class. Each student distracts, reacts, or causes a commotion even before class has started. The teacher redirects the behaviors until all students are seated and paying attention. Once the teacher begins the lesson, students ask absurd questions, ask to be excused, explain why the information does not pertain to their situations, or are generally off-task.

Everyone gets a good laugh and it feels like a catharsis for the teachers participating in the skit. They are able to laugh at the most tragic, draining, and absurd part of their jobs—managing adults who can be very unmanageable.

If a teacher becomes an adult education teacher to avoid having to manage students, that teacher is in for a harsh reality check. Adults are people just like children and like children have their own quirks, needs, and issues which a teacher must manage to have a successful classroom.

Many adult learners return to the educational setting reluctantly, as a means to an end. They return because they may have hit the "glass ceiling" in the workplace due to a lack of education. They return because they have been ordered by the courts to take courses. They may return because they want to improve their situation but are still fearful and prepared to quit at the first sign that they may not be successful.[1]

In all these cases, it will take a teacher skilled in working with adults and in managing their unique behaviors in the classroom to ensure that students are successful. Teachers must understand how emotions that students bring with them into the classroom will affect their ability to learn, how the timing of presenting new materials is essential for student engagement, how honoring all student experiences will entice students to be motivated to participate in class in meaningful ways, and how providing the appropriate amount of support with the optimal amount of challenge will increase student success in the class.

THE ROLE OF EMOTIONS

Jennie came to class with dirt under her fingernails, her hair matted to the back of her head, dirty clothes, stomach grumbling, and a black eye. The teacher greeted her, but Jennie avoided eye contact. She signed in and took her seat in front of a computer, logging into the day's lessons. About an hour later she called the teacher over.

"I've been blocked," she told the teacher, staring straight ahead at the computer.

"Okay, I'll unblock you. Do you want some help?" the teacher offered.

"No," Jennie responded flatly.

She left early that day and when the teacher checked at the end of the day for students who were blocked out of the curriculum for missing too many questions—a computer's method for ensuring students seek extra help when needed—Jennie was on the list. The teacher hoped that by tomorrow Jennie was feeling better. The teacher wrote herself a note to offer Jennie help again, this time a bit more insistently.

It may be such common knowledge as to border on being a cliché among educators, but according to Maslow's hierarchy, if a student's basic needs, such as food, clothing, and safety, aren't met, then very little learning will occur.

What does that mean for an educator of adult at-risk students? Teachers recognize that often adult students' situations are caused by their choices; their needs are going unmet because of their actions. Regardless of why students' needs are unmet and whether as educators we feel sympathy or irritation toward them and their plight, unmet needs translate into a student's inability to focus on learning.

Teachers cannot control what happens outside of the classroom. Teachers must focus on what can be done while students are inside the classroom—creating a comfortable environment which meets students' physiological needs, their safety needs, their need to belong, and their esteem needs.

To meet the needs of students biologically and physiologically means to provide for them in ways which prepare them for learning. This does not mean that one should feed, clothe, or provide students with hygiene products, nor should a teacher provide medical attention or give nutritional advice. Instead teachers must provide for students the things to be expected in a school setting.

Making sure the drinking fountain and bathrooms are accessible and in working order for students should be the responsibility of the school or host facility, but it is a good idea to check on those things for students. Also ensuring that the classroom has proper ventilation and temperature as well as safe furniture and adequate supplies is a way a teacher can be proactive for students.

Many adult educators allow for a coffee or tea area that students stock. This allows students to have a warm cup of coffee or tea and sends the message that they are full humans in this setting. These simple measures can go a long way toward helping students concentrate on learning rather than worrying about being uncomfortable.

Preparing adults for learning by beginning each lesson with some time to de-stress from family or work allows students to get in a positive emotional state for learning. Allowing time for settling in and socializing at the beginning of class and beginning instruction with an anticipatory set that allows for student engagement and success, and even humor if possible, create routines and alleviate stress.

Creating a safe zone in a classroom can be rather tricky but is worth the effort. A teacher's most powerful tool is his or her presence. The example a teacher sets through actions, responses to students, encouragement for participation, and discouragement of inappropriate behavior will set the tone in the classroom for a safe learning environment. Being a good role model is the greatest free resource available to teachers.[2]

By modeling the behavior and language of the mainstream middle-class culture, teachers provide students with practice and an emotional comfort level with these new language and behavior norms until the student is able to transfer these behaviors beyond the classroom. Teachers are usually powerless to motivate a student to attempt this transition. Instead a student is encouraged to change because his or her current situation is too painful to stay in.[3] Recognizing this pain and helping the student make a successful change by modeling that success can be very rewarding.

Providing students with regular, predictable breaks prevents student discomfort and allows students to feel that while in class, their basic needs are being met and accommodated for. Being in a predictable environment and having a teacher who has taken the time to be sure that the simple necessities are taken care of creates an environment of safety, Maslow's second level of need.

Creating a positive tone the first few days of class is easy. Students are eager, have signed up to gain skills, and have hope that they will be successful. But as the weeks wear on, many students are confronted with the same struggles that caused them to not finish school, to not complete their degree, or to repeat the class. Some of these students will quietly stop coming to class. Others may turn their frustration onto the teacher or may direct that frustration onto other students.

Teachers, as the role models of behavior for the class, must be vigilant in the creation of a positive environment.

A first important step is for teachers to always assume there is a good reason for what may be perceived as misbehavior. In one class, there was a student who was writing the entire time the teacher was instructing. He rarely looked up at the teacher. He never looked at the board, even when the teacher emphatically made a point of writing a key idea on it. He even continued writing while his classmates engaged in the class discussion. The teacher stood near him. He kept writing. The teacher stood across from him and caught his fleeting glance. He kept writing. Finally, the teacher called his name.

"Joseph, are you with us?"

"Yes." He looked up at the teacher just long enough to answer, then put his head down and started writing again. The teacher sighed and moved on with class. The teacher acknowledged that Joseph was an adult and obviously had something more important than class going on in his life. The teacher assumed Joseph would not be off-task unless he had an urgent need to write someone a letter. The teacher didn't blame the student, just accepted it. She did decide that she would talk to him individually after class.

At the class's break, everyone left the room. Once everyone was gone, the teacher walked over to Joseph's desk and looked at what he had been writing.

To her astonishment, Joseph had been transcribing everything the teacher and his classmates said. Now, this is not the most effective way to take notes, but despite all the evidence that Joseph was off-task, he was definitely on-task. Imagine the disaster if Joseph had been confronted and accused of being off-task. He would have had to defend himself. The teacher would have been exposed as a teacher who doesn't trust her students and may have lost the respect of many of the students. This was one classroom management disaster narrowly missed.

In his book, *Coping with Misconduct in the College Classroom*, Gerald Amada provides teachers with a variety of behaviors that could be construed as misbehavior and a variety of strategies for dealing with them. The most important management strategy he provides is to check with the student privately to be sure that your perception of the misbehavior is correct. He points out that if a student was actually being disruptive or acting out, by handling the situation privately and in a positive manner, the behavior will usually quickly vanish.[4]

It is not okay to ignore bad behavior in a classroom. This sends a message to the other students that the teacher is not in charge and does not take his job seriously enough to create a serious learning environment. By making the information and curriculum relevant to students' lives and honoring all student engagement, the teacher will set a positive tone for all learning. If students come to class and feel positive, the brain becomes aroused, focusing attention, memory, and higher thinking skills on the learning.[5]

Basic behavior modification theory states that to change a person's behavior, the feedback should be two positive comments to every one negative comment.[6] For example, if a student provides a wrong answer in class, the teacher can provide positive feedback by acknowledging that the student took a risk by answering the question in front of the entire class. The teacher can provide positive feedback about the understanding the student has exhibited thus far. This allows the student to be receptive to the fact that she answered incorrectly and to hear why rather than to shut down and believe learning the material is too difficult.

Teachers have opportunities to reframe situations that may be perceived as negative to positive. Rather than allowing the student to overgeneralize, "I'm no good at this," the teacher has an opportunity to explain to the student how he came to the wrong answer and how to get to the correct answer.

Acknowledging the progress the student has made so far in learning the new material and framing the situation as "This was a difficult task but you can do it" helps encourage the student to continue to tackle the material.[7] Through the 2:1 ratio of positive feedback to negative feedback, teachers create positive perceptions about the ability of students and the accessibility of the curriculum.

Research has documented that teachers shape the emotional intelligence of our students by helping them to attain goals and manage negative emotions.[8] When students feel a teacher's correction is negative, the middle brain goes into fight-or-flight mode and prohibits the corrected information from reaching the thinking brain; the brain is too busy trying to preserve self-integrity.[9] But when teachers acknowledge the progress a student is making and how taking risks is the best way to learn new material, the teacher creates a sense of success in the student.

Even when the teacher sets a positive example, there may be times when the safety of the classroom is compromised by students. If a student answers a question and the other students in the class react in a negative manner, this may threaten the student who answered. It is important to quickly model appropriate behavior for those students who have reacted negatively while addressing the student who feels threatened.

By providing a context for the wrong answer, students see how anyone in class could have made the mistake. "That's an easy mistake to make because . . ." or "When I first learned this I was confused by . . ." These statements create an environment in which failure is accepted as part of learning and risk taking is encouraged. It corrects the negative reaction to a wrong answer and models an appropriate way to respond to a wrong answer.

Teachers will know when a student has felt threatened and the safety of the classroom has been compromised by observing the student. If a student has her fists closed, puts hands on her hips, begins pointing, starts wringing her hands, crosses her arms, or begins to fidget, the student likely has felt threatened.[10] It is important to reestablish a feeling of safety for the student by focusing the student on positive cues.

"Thank you for risking an answer" may work, but the teacher may need to be more direct with the student without further threatening her. Asking clarifying questions that allow the student to express why she is feeling threatened may work. Providing open-ended prompts such as "Explain to me how you got to that answer" will encourage students to explore their thinking and acknowledge what they have mastered thus far.

If a student refuses to engage in further discussion, it is important to move on and approach the student privately later. If the student's brain has downshifted to survival mode and stress hormones have been released, no amount of coaxing on the teacher's part will get her to engage at that moment.[11]

The best classroom management technique is to wait until the student has had time to process the feelings, then to begin again. Talking to the student privately after some time has passed and reframing the incident for her in a positive manner allows the release of neurotransmitters into the brain and the student to once again focus her attention.

As a teacher of adults, it is important to recognize that emotional memories are extremely influential in students' learning process.[12] By linking positive emotions to curriculum, the teacher will help students to learn.

TIMING IS EVERYTHING

Humans are most uncomfortable when they do not know what to expect. One productive thing teachers can do for students is to provide a predictable classroom routine. The lower brain is able to turn over control to the higher thinking areas of the brain when it knows what to expect.[13]

A classroom routine that provides time to settle in, time to preview what to expect for the class's session, time to take in new information, time to safely practice with the new information, time to summarize, and time to extend learning beyond the current lesson is the most productive use of classroom time.[14] These positive and productive routines provide the brain the predictability needed to focus on learning new information.

As the teacher, taking the time to greet students individually and making eye contact with each student creates an environment of safety and welcome. This also allows teachers to take stock of how students are doing emotionally. Being aware of the students' emotions allows the teacher to time periods of success and safety with periods of challenge and struggle.

The adult classroom may have instructional periods of three hours. As the teacher, if there isn't a set break time, it is important to allow for at least one official break taken every class meeting at a predictable time so students can plan for the time to rest and revive. There is a 5–15 percent increase in blood and oxygen flow to the brain when a student stands; integrating breaks and opportunities for physical movement will create a more aroused and alert student.

Insisting that all students get up and move about, even by leaving the classroom yourself or by calling students who stay behind and hang out at their desks up to the teacher's desk to check in will create students who come back from break refreshed. Breaks should be at least twenty minutes long, and students should not be required to sustain attention for more than a forty-five-minute stretch.

It is also important to allow time for reflection in the classroom.[15] One technique is to be sure that lectures do not last for more than ten minutes at a time. After ten minutes, allow students two minutes to either discuss the topic with a partner, do a quick write-up about how the information pertains to them, or simply quietly think about the information. These two minutes of reflection allow the brain to connect the new information to previously learned information, thus creating a path to store and retrieve the information.

Often it is said in the adult classroom that students learn more from each other than they will from the teacher. It is not that students have more knowledge or expertise than the teacher, but students model for other students how to integrate the instructor's knowledge and expertise into their knowledge base. Allowing students time to explain what the information means to them provides other students with opportunities to integrate the knowledge in the same manner or with models of how the information could be applicable to them.

As the teacher, taking the time to provide feedback that confirms progress, discusses concerns, and provides input into the process of integrating the information in the students' knowledge base[16] is time well spent. Interacting with students by affirming their successes allows the teacher to build self-esteem in students so that when it is time to challenge them, to provide them with opportunities to stretch their abilities and take risks, they will trust that they can make attempts without fearing humiliation.

Students learn at different speeds. It is natural for students to be anxious or nervous when faced with a new learning situation.[17] By building trust with students, providing a predictable environment, and creating a safe environment for risk taking through modeling and positive reinforcement, the teacher will be able to time moments for risk taking and challenges in the curriculum to fit students' needs.

After formal instruction of new material ends, providing students with opportunities to integrate that new information with choices allows them to control their level of engagement, challenge, and risk taking. When an adult learner has control over the nature, timing, and direction of the learning process, the entire experience is facilitated. Choices such as group work, providing a variety of assignments to choose from, or allowing students to create their own applications of the new material will provide students the control necessary for optimal engagement.

Teachers must be careful about assuming that because last week a student took a huge risk in class, the student will always take those kinds of risks. Motivation is fluid, constantly changing, and the teacher's evaluation of a student's level of motivation will usually be wrong.[18] Teachers must be sure to see their role, after providing formal instruction, as that of a facilitator to learning for students, not the director. Having students choose a relevant application of the knowledge gained in class allows students to take ownership of the new information.

Being able to provide consistent timing of classroom routines and procedures, as well as providing flexible timing for challenging students, is important in a classroom filled with at-risk adults. Too many adult students bring negative school experiences with them.

It seems unfair to ask adult education teachers to help students overcome some cruel, flippant remark a second-grade teacher made or the ridicule a student endured at the hands of her tenth-grade biology teacher when she spelled a word wrong on the board. But if adult education teachers do not make the effort to do so, they may be added to that long list of reasons why this adult is not successful in school.

HONOR ALL EXPERIENCES

Many educators go into adult education because they believe it will be easy. No hall monitoring, no parents to deal with, no hormones to contend with, no Back-to-School Nights to host. What many educators find when teaching adults is that there are other challenges, such as adults who have their own experiences and perceptions that could challenge the teacher's authority.

To establish authority in class, it is important to set out clear classroom expectations each time students meet. By creating an environment in which students know what is expected of them, they will be able and generally willing to meet those expectations.[19] Teachers must be sure that the expectations also honor the experiences and perceptions that students bring into the classroom.

Let's look at the variety of experiences that may be present in a class of at-risk adults. In one class there may be a man who was a Vietnam veteran, a Vietnamese-American having moved to the United States and becoming a citizen after the Vietnam War; a man who grew up homeless with his drug-addicted mother; a grandfather of twelve; and fifteen other unique students with unique backgrounds.

What brings such a wide range of people together is the desire for information that will improve their lives. That desire, though, is coupled with the students' own established values, beliefs, and opinions. As the teacher it is important to understand that if the students' values, beliefs, or opinions are threatened in such a way as to destroy a sense of safety, then being able to focus on learning new information will not be possible. It may be a challenge to allow for diverse student background knowledge and experiences to influence the learning process in a class with such a variety of students, but the dividends are worth the effort.

The adult brain creates meaning by linking past to present into familiar patterns.[20] Students will be constantly seeking ways to attach the new information presented to information they already have. This desire for connection can manifest itself in ways which could be perceived as challenging to the teacher's authority.

In one class, the teacher was reviewing stress reduction techniques as part of an anger management lesson. The technique being practiced was visualization and the teacher had asked the students to close their eyes as he read aloud from a script about a peaceful, beautiful place. There were several students who refused to close their eyes and participate, actually fidgeting the entire time. The teacher stood near them but did not address their nonparticipation, realizing this would have been disruptive to the intent of reducing stress.

Once the exercise was over, the teacher asked for input as to how the technique worked for students. One of the students who had refused to participate raised his hand.

"That stuff doesn't work for me," he said.

The teacher smiled and asked, "What does work for you?"

"Nothing," the student answered, frowning and turning his body away from the front of the class.

It would have been very easy for the teacher to point out that the student hadn't even tried the visualization technique so he couldn't know if it worked. But pointing this out could have been perceived as a confrontation of what the student felt he knew.

"Well," the teacher began slowly, "today and tomorrow you will be introduced to several different ways of dealing with stress. Remember to check in with me at the end of tomorrow's lesson to let me know which tools you think could work for you."

The student nodded and the class moved on.

The teacher was able to respect the student's experience by asking him what does work for him while providing an opportunity for him and for all students to be open to the variety of tools for managing stress that were going to be presented in class.

Learning is tightly connected to a student's background knowledge and experience. Teachers should acknowledge this by drawing out a student's experiences and knowledge and creating narratives for the students to show how their experiences are relevant to the topic. The students' knowledge and experience to add greatly to the value of the class. [21]

In the previous example, the student claimed to not have any experience with dealing with stress. More likely, he didn't yet have the ability to articulate his experience for the teacher, class, and himself. When the teacher asked him to check back in later, the teacher allowed him an opportunity to articulate, or create a narrative, to master the information presented in the curriculum in a personally meaningful manner.

As previously mentioned, a good teacher allows students to learn from each other during practice and processing of new information. Student narratives about how they make sense of new information allow other students to see that they are makers of meaning and constructors of knowledge. Through teacher support and guidance, students can make meaning in ways that have the potential to change their perspectives. [22]

A teacher challenges and supports students in this endeavor by honoring multiple perspectives. When messages or newly formed ideas are inconsistent with personal experience and values, they are quickly forgotten and filtered out. But people retain and apply information in meaningful ways when that information is connected to real-life experiences. [23]

Holding class discussions allowing students to share how the new information presented in class connects to something they already know provides opportunities for students to make connections and to witness other students making meaning out of the information. Teachers are responsible for guiding the discussion to be inclusive of all experiences and to allow each student to create a narrative to integrate the new information into his or her experience.

A teacher can ask questions such as "Does this make sense to you? How?" She can prompt students by saying "Tell me a time when you may have experienced this and didn't really know what it was." This provides opportunities for student articulation of the new information.

Just as all things in nature appear connected to something else, our brain is a "connection of neurons." [24] By allowing students to connect new information presented in class to experiences and information they already have, the brain is making powerful connections and pathways for storage and retrieval of the new information.

SUPPORT AND CHALLENGE

This chapter has examined the need to make students feel safe in the classroom. Once a sense of safety has been established through predictable routines, a sense of inclusion, and appropriate timing of assignments, it is appropriate to challenge students.

If a student does not feel supported in class and is challenged by the curriculum, that student will retreat. If a student is given lots of support but not adequately challenged, the student retains her status quo and no growth is accomplished. It is the balance of appropriate support and appropriate curriculum that results in significant growth for the student.[25]

When a student is challenged without the appropriate support, the student will feel threatened or anxious and learning will cease. If teachers are aware of the signals students provide, they will be able to make accommodations for all students and provide adequate support for them to meet the curricular challenges of the class. Support can begin with simple respect. If students know that they and their experiences are honored and respected, they are more likely to feel supported and willing to take risks with curricular challenges. The easiest way to show respect is to build rapport with students through physical proximity and psychological proximity.[26]

The days of "the sage on the stage" are long gone. It is important during class discussions, group work, and practice time for the teacher to circulate throughout the room and show students that though the teacher may be providing instruction, he is also part of the community of learners in the class. If the teacher simply sits down to join a group during group work, students will feel more at ease with his presence. By engaging students during practice time and providing support or affirmations, students will learn to trust that the teacher's mission in class is to support them.

Likewise, by creating an appropriate familiarity with students, remembering their names and key attributes of their lives, the teacher can create an environment of trust and respect.[27] The more students trust the teacher with the details of their lives, the more they will trust him to support them during challenging times of the curricular sequence.

Another important step to creating an environment of support is through providing opportunities for early success. When students experience success early in class, they begin a narrative about "this class" wherein they see themselves as capable. This vision of themselves allows them to tackle more difficult problems later in class.[28]

Balancing support with curricular challenge is the art of being a teacher. Through early achievements in class, a student develops a sense of persistence when tasks grow increasingly more difficult. Creating this sense of accomplishment through specific praise for positive achievements[29] should be the goal of all teachers. This sense of accomplishment allows teachers to then set difficult tasks before students with the assurance that students will attempt to meet the high expectations set for them.

Finally, allowing students to deviate from the prescribed lesson and to find their own direction to meet the goals of the lesson allows the lesson to meet all learner needs. To be allowed this flexibility creates a sense of trust that the teacher is more concerned with the students' success than with the lesson plan or assignment.[30] Providing the goal of the lesson, then allowing students to create their own path to meet that goal, gives students a sense of ownership of the material and allows them to see the teacher in a supporting role.

Research shows that the most positive influence on the brain's chemical composition is positive feedback. Positive feedback is a necessary part of a healthy self-concept[31] and creates a sense of support in the classroom. When students are reassured that the path they have chosen, with the teacher's guidance, to complete the goals of the curriculum is worthwhile, this is positive feedback about their abilities in class and their abilities to manage their learning.

Challenging students requires being very explicit about the goals for the classroom. The movie *Stand and Deliver* is a great example of setting very high expectations for students, then providing support for students to be able to meet these expectations. Teacher Jaime Escalante doesn't shelter students from high expectations, nor does he prescribe how students will get there. He simply states what the expectations are—to pass the AP exam—and then works with students to get them there.

By beginning a class with a clear goal or high expectations, the teacher is able to allow students some self-direction. When given choice, students will work in learning modalities that are their strengths and choose an appropriate level of difficulty for themselves. By honoring these choices, the teacher provides the necessary support and challenges students to meet the goal in their own unique way.

The teacher's job during the course of a classroom curriculum is to provide the appropriate level of difficulty, provide the appropriate level of support, and decrease barriers to student success.

Do you remember the nursery rhymes we all learned as children? They felt like play, but we were actually learning—to count, to recite our ABCs, to learn our colors. Likewise, in the adult education classroom, the teacher will want to introduce play as one of the learning strategies. Play establishes pathways from the part of your brain that makes decisions and needs support to tackle challenges to the part of the brain that creates a sense of well-being; this positive experience is directly related to memory and performance.[32]

Later chapters will examine ways to provide your students choices within a curricular unit.

CONCLUSION

Managing the at-risk adult learner is about creating a healthy classroom. The first step is creating a physically healthy classroom, with proper ventilation, cleanliness, and safety. The second step is creating a psychologically healthy classroom through appropriate boundaries, high expectations, a supportive and welcoming climate, and mutual respect between teacher and learner.

When adults are asked which classrooms and teachers they most enjoyed, the overwhelming answer is those classrooms in which they felt valued and respected. As teachers of this unique population, it is important to remember that our job is to facilitate a future for students that is brighter than their past.

POINTS TO REMEMBER

- Students' positive emotions toward school can be improved by ensuring a safe and stable classroom experience.
- Teachers must be careful not to assume misbehavior when students act outside of the classroom norms.
- Providing positive feedback enhances student classroom success.
- Predictable routines in class help students concentrate on the presented curriculum.
- Beginning classroom routines help students prepare to learn.
- Regular predictable instructional pacing helps students focus.
- Honoring all student experiences enriches the learning environment.
- Teachers must balance support and challenge for students.
- Creating appropriate familiarity with students increases their engagement with the curriculum.
- Allowing student choice in demonstrating mastery of the curriculum increases motivation.

NOTES

1. "Adults Returning to School," The College Info Center, http://www.collegeinfo.org/adults.pdf.

2. Ruby K. Payne, *A Framework for Understanding Poverty* (Highlands, TX: aha! Process Inc., 1996), 67.

3. Stanton Samenow, *Inside the Criminal Mind* (New York: Crown, 2004), 154.

4. Gerald Amada, *Coping with Misconduct in the College Classroom* (St. Johns, FL: College Administration Publications, 1999), 74–77.

5. Laurie Materna, *Jump Start the Adult Learner: How to Engage and Motivate Adults Using Brain-Compatible Strategies* (Thousand Oaks, CA: Corwin Press, 2007), 71.

6. Jeffery A. Cantor, *Delivering Instruction to Adult Learners* (Toronto: Wall & Emerson, 1992), 40.

7. Martin E. P. Seligman, *Learned Optimism: How to Change Your Mind and Your Life* (New York: Vantage Books, 2006), 142–146.

8. Joseph E. Zins, Roger P. Weissberg, Margaret C. Wang, and Herbert J. Walberg, *Building Academic Success on Social and Emotional Learning: What Does the Research Say?* (New York: Teachers College Press, 2004), 168–172.

9. Payne, *Framework for Understanding Poverty*, 64.

10. Cantor, *Delivering Instruction to Adult Learners*, 207.

11. Materna, *Jump Start the Adult Learner*, 11.

12. Materna, *Jump Start the Adult Learner*, 9.

13. Materna, *Jump Start the Adult Learner*, 6–7.

14. "Classroom Routines: A Must!" About.com, http://specialed.about.com/cs/ teacherstrategies/a/routines.htm.

15. Materna, *Jump Start the Adult Learner*, 162.

16. Cantor, *Delivering Instruction to Adult Learners*, 43–44.

17. Mel Levine, *One Mind at a Time* (New York: Simon and Schuster, 2002), 265–266.

18. Levine, *One Mind at a Time*, 263–264.

19. Payne, *Framework for Understanding Poverty*, 107–108.

20. Materna, *Jump Start the Adult Learner*, 19.

21. Materna, *Jump Start the Adult Learner*, 52–53.

22. Zins et al., *Building Academic Success*, 168–172.

23. Cantor, *Delivering Instruction to Adult Learners*, 152.

24. Robert Sylwester, *A Celebration of Neurons: An Educator's Guide to the Brain* (Alexandria, VA: Association for Supervision and Curriculum Development, 1995), 121–125.

25. Laurent A. Daloz, *Effective Teaching and Mentoring* (San Francisco: Jossey-Bass, 1986), 162.

26. Cantor, *Delivering Instruction to Adult Learners*, 156.

27. "A Teacher's Guide to Earning Student Respect," Youth Rights, http://www.youthrights.net/index.php?title=A_Teachers_Guide_on_Earning_Student_Respect.

28. Cantor, *Delivering Instruction to Adult Learners*, 156.

29. Hendrie Weisinger, *The Power of Positive Criticism* (New York: Amacom, 2000), 86–88.

30. Cantor, *Delivering Instruction to Adult Learners*, 153.

31. Robert Sylwester, "The neurobiology of self-esteem and aggression," *Educational Leadership* 54 (1997): 75–79.

32. Materna, *Jump Start the Adult Learner*, 85.

SEVEN

Classroom Environment

When teachers think of creating a classroom environment, many think of elementary school, the beautiful bulletin boards, and postings of student work. Teachers of adults rarely engage in these types of displays, often because unlike in elementary school, they are not assigned their own classrooms. Instead adult educators conduct classes held at various classrooms that are shared with other teachers.

Adult education teachers sometimes believe bulletin boards and postings of student work are "elementary" and adults don't need or want these types of stimuli in the classroom. But, there is more to the classroom environment than bulletin boards and postings of student work.

Beyond colorful walls, considering classroom environment includes considering a student's affective filter or how students will react when entering a classroom. Adult students, especially those at risk, thrive in a learning environment that is risk free and filled with authentic communication between the teacher and students and among students. Creating a risk-free classroom environment includes paying attention to the emotional tone of the classroom, the use of the physical space in the classroom, and the use of technology in the classroom.

PREDICTABLE ROUTINES

Brain research shows that when students are distracted by guessing what the teacher will do next in class or what they will be expected to do, they are not able to give full attention to the concepts being presented.[1] But when the student is involved in an environment that is predictable and safe, the brain is able to fully concentrate on learning.

Routines make a student's experience in the classroom predictable. The first important routine is to begin starting class the same way each day. Many teachers begin the class with a ritual greeting and a warm-up activity that includes either a review of the previous lesson or an introduction to the day's lesson.

In Gina's classroom, there is always a brainteaser projected at the front of the class that students can work on individually or with partners. Not only does the brainteaser review or introduce concepts in the class, but it gives Gina time to take roll, interact individually with students to handle any concerns that might interfere with their ability to concentrate, and check in with students as they are working on the problem. Often Gina gives hints for solving the brainteaser to keep students motivated. The brainteasers are fun, so the stress level is minimal while engaging.

Another important routine is to end class the same way each day. Many teachers have "packing up" routines that signal to the class that instructional time is over. Packing up routines can include copying the reading or homework assignment from the board into a planner or student choral responses to end-of-class questions. Having students copy assignments due and future due dates helps them to plan a work schedule for completion of larger assignments.

Other teachers use the same lesson closure each class, such as checking for understanding. Ending class this way helps the students review the lesson and provides valuable feedback to the teacher about the success of the lesson. One great checking-for-understanding technique is for students to complete an "out-the-door ticket": the teacher asks a comprehension question that students answer on a piece of paper and turn in as they are leaving the class.

Instructional strategies routines help students focus more on the subject matter being learned than on the classroom expectations. Students who are struggling to understand what the teacher wants them to do are unable to focus on what the teacher wants them to learn. When teachers identify a strategy that best meets the needs of the instructional intent and the unique classroom population and then model how it is used, the strategy quickly becomes a routine in the classroom.

In a literacy classroom, students routinely progress through a series of higher-level-thinking questions about a text and then summarize the text. The format for this introduction strategy was modeled early in the class and the students have become familiar with it. Because of this familiarity, they are able to spend their intellectual energy on deciphering the text rather than deciphering the questions and expectations.

When introducing an instructional strategy, it is important to create routines surrounding the strategy. By evaluating the routines, the teacher can determine which are most successful and reuse them when introducing other instructional strategies. Teachers should closely monitor student success with the new strategy. If students appear to be struggling, the teacher can use one of several interventions to help them.

One intervention is to guide students through verbal mediation or self-dialogue, a metacognition strategy reviewed in the next chapter. A dialogue might include: What am I being asked to do? Do I understand? Have I completed the task successfully? What do I do next?

Another teacher intervention is to restate the directions with more precise language if more than one student has asked for the same clarification. If two students have asked for the same clarification, then it is reasonable to assume that there are more students in class who are confused about specific expectations of the assignment. For example, clarifications as simple as answering the questions in full sentences or full paragraphs may need to be repeated.

Other possible strategies include gentle teacher reminders throughout the lesson about which part of the routine students should be performing and what that routine should look like. By reminding students how their progress should look at timed intervals, teachers help students to plan their learning time for completion of the assignment. By stopping at important milestones during the assignment and showing students what the assignment could look like by holding up a successful student's work, you validate the student work and give a model for other students to use as guidance for their work.

Often when students are completing routine assignments, they will have clarification questions. The manner in which the teacher handles these interactions goes a long way in creating the emotional classroom environment. It is important that when a teacher is handling student responses, the teacher provides feedback that is descriptive and not evaluative. Authentic communication begins with clear expectations.

For example, approaching a student and informing him that he is "doing it all wrong" is the fastest way to get most students to give up. But if the teacher sees her role as a resource, not the expert, she might ask the students, "Explain to me where you are in the assignment." This allows the teacher to act as coach or mentor rather than as the expert.

One good-mannered routine is to stick to organized breaks. Predictable breaks allow all students the mental break they need, but also allow time for those students who need to get out of the class to be able to refocus.

Creating routines connected with lesson flow helps students to build academic stamina by setting up timed periods of concentrated efforts to listen interspersed with time for practice and reflection on the information being presented. Lesson-timing routines allow students to predict how long they need to sustain attention. For example, if teachers prepare checking-for-understanding questions to use after each block of instructional time, students can predict the routine and be prepared mentally for the questions.

A wait-time routine is time that is built into the structure of a lesson in order to allow the class to think and listen before responding. Teachers pose questions and routinely provide "wait time," thirty seconds to a full minute, before calling on students to share. Wait-time routines create an environment that values all student responses and encourages all students to think deeply about questions posed by the teacher.

These are all classroom routines that the teacher can promote, but good students must have self-initiated routines outside of the classroom to be successful in school. Teachers can promote these beyond classroom routines in several ways.

One out-of-class routine that a teacher can encourage is for students to keep a daily planner where they record class topics, assignments, and important dates. Most teachers provide a syllabus that forms the backbone of a student's planner; requiring students to then transcribe the syllabus into their personal planner creates a routine that will carry beyond the classroom. A daily planner will also help students anticipate deadlines, and if the teacher posts upcoming due dates, this will create the routine of anticipating time left to complete an assignment.

Another out-of-class routine that teachers can encourage is one geared toward turning in assignments on time. If a large assignment is due, teachers can require students to turn in progress reports along the way. This helps students to anticipate deadlines by completing work in sections. Finally, providing students with a manageable workload for the class is important. Teachers must remember that adult students have outside commitments and one major reason for at-risk students to not persist is the interference of other responsibilities.

Classroom environment does include classroom management, even for adults. It is important to remember to manage the behavior not the person. For example, it seems common sense that students should not be out of their seats during instructional time, but there are many students who need to be reminded of this. By treating the behavior as a misunderstanding of a routine rather than as a time to punish bad behavior, the classroom environment becomes a nonthreatening environment. When a teacher stops instruction and states, "It is inappropriate to be out of your seat during instructional time," she is managing the behavior by reinforcing behavioral routines.

In conclusion, by providing students routines and a predictable environment within the classroom, teachers help to prepare students to be available intellectually for the work to be completed in the classroom.

MOTIVATION

Having predictable routines will allow students to feel comfortable, which supports the ultimate goal for a teacher: to motivate students to do their best.

The teacher's motivation for teaching a concept sets the tone for the lesson. If the teacher approaches the lesson with an attitude of "I have to teach you this," students will be less than motivated. If a teacher is excited about being able to teach students new material, then students will pick up on the teacher's attitude and the tone of the classroom environment will be one of contagious motivation. Teachers who are truly interested in their subject set an example for students for why the subject is interesting and worth learning about.

Adults are most motivated when they see relevance in the material being taught.[2] If an adult student can easily see how the material is going to improve their lives—whether at work, at home, or socially—they will be motivated. It is a good idea for teachers to show students how the material is relevant to their lives and to allow students to share with one another why the material will improve their lives.

As mentioned in previous chapters, a great place to allow students to see how the lesson will improve their lives is during the anticipatory set when students are making connections between the new material and prior knowledge or previous experiences. A teacher can also show students how the information is relevant to their lives in setting up the guided practice or independent practice with the new knowledge that includes application to student lives.

For example, in an adult education class on managing real estate, the teacher brought in the local newspaper's classified section, a local home magazine, and a computer for access to Craigslist. Students were given the task of using a spreadsheet for comparing properties being advertised, then as homework they were to go home and "value" their current residence. The assignment was a real-world application of the information and allowed students to see how with the information they could make wise choices about real estate in the future.

Unfortunately, motivation can diminish if students feel they will be unable to master the material. Thus, the teacher must be sure to differentiate instruction so each student is learning at an appropriate level of difficulty. One easy way to differentiate instruction is to give adults a choice in how to demonstrate mastery of the material.

For example, in an early childhood development class, for the culminating project students were given the choice of either writing a traditional research paper, presenting a PowerPoint display to the class on a key concept, conducting a research project and presenting a "science fair" display, or creating an early childhood unit to be implemented at a local preschool. The choices allowed students to work in the medium they were most comfortable, utilizing their talents and following their interests.

Another form of differentiation is to allow student interaction in the class where students are able to work together to complete classwork and assignments. Having students work in cooperative groups to complete a project will increase motivation because each student recognizes that not all the responsibility falls on his shoulders while at the same time it is imperative for him to complete the assigned portion of the project since other students are counting on him or her.

Finally, humor in the class can increase motivation.[3] Beginning a lesson with a comic or appropriate joke can set a positive tone and allows for everyone to begin the class with a stress reliever. It is important to let humor fit your personality and to fit the instructional concepts. Mario, a veteran teacher of automotive repair, collects comic strips about car repairs and routinely uses them in class to lighten the mood, especially when the lesson is a challenging one. But be cautious of using humor at the expense of students. Sarcasm is always inappropriate in the classroom and private humor creates a classroom environment of insiders and outsiders, not something everyone is participating in.

Student motivation is an important ingredient when creating an environment that allows all students success. Motivating students does not happen without teacher motivation.

VISUALS

Part of creating the classroom environment is choosing what visuals to use for enhancing student engagement. Many adult educators have very little control over the space where classes are held, often teaching in several different classrooms for different topics. Even in these cases, the teacher can use visuals to create a positive classroom environment.

One important step to gaining student attention for the lesson is in creating a classroom environment that is not distracting. Eliminating distractions can mean covering windows that look out on a busy student area or editing decorations and bulletin boards. Teachers want to be sure that students are focused on the lesson, not on what is happening outside the window in the student area.

Creating a positive classroom environment can be as easy as posting examples of successful uses of the instructional concepts being taught.[4] Of course, simple motivation posters promote success such as the poster of the kitten hanging on with the caption "Hang in there." Another way to keep motivation high and student attitudes positive is to use posters of successful people in the area you are teaching. In a writing class, posting pictures of famous authors and what they say about writing allows for students to be familiar with others who have undertaken similar academic endeavors and been successful.

With other subjects, choosing famous and maybe not-so-famous but still successful people and sharing these images with students will help them see how they can be successful in the content area. One teacher has a bulletin board of pictures of past graduates from her program. These pictures allow current students to visualize successful completion of the coursework and to be motivated to have their pictures added to the wall.

Using the walls of your classroom to set the theme for a unit of study is another way to create a positive and motivating classroom environment. The use of peripherals sets the theme of the new unit of study, actively engages learners, and keeps their attention focused on the topic.

In a fundamentals of writing class, the lesson was about writing an essay by building paragraphs together into a coherent argument. The teacher brought in a series of paper "bricks" and modeled how the writer must lay a foundation of shared knowledge by placing bricks with key vocabulary and definitions as well as shared experiences on the bottom row. Then the teacher placed bricks upon this foundation that represented the tenets of the argument, stopping each time to explain how the foundation allows her to make the argument.

Finally, the top brick was the thesis. The bricks not only set the theme of the unit—building an argument—but also provided an analogy for thinking about the unit and provided students kinesthetic practice when they "built" their own arguments out of the bricks given to them.

Another excellent way to share visuals with the class without having to bring in bins of stuff is to have students bring in artifacts related to the topic. Much like "show and tell" in grade school, this allows learners to connect to the topic personally and takes some of the burden of creating a stimulating classroom environment off of the teacher. In Carla's classroom, when she begins teaching the unit on metric measurement of liquids, she has students bring in recipes, drinks, and canned goods to demonstrate not only the theme of the unit but also how learning the material will apply to their lives.

Finally, the easiest way to use visuals in the classroom is to post learner-generated posters and mind maps. Creating posters, either with partners or in groups, as a culminating exercise when students have learned a new concept not only makes the concept personally meaningful to the learners but also helps to create a stimulating learning environment through the use of visuals.

TECHNOLOGY

Today, a key component in any classroom environment is how technology is integrated. Many times the teacher has little control over the environment, especially over which technologies are available in the classroom. Nonetheless, it is crucial to find a way to integrate technology in the classroom environment. Technological proficiency will help students in their daily lives for things such as budgeting or letter writing. It also will help them when in the job market, as most jobs require some degree of technological knowledge, even jobs such as cashier, clerical worker, or mechanic. Adults with technological skills have significant advantages in the job market.[5]

To integrate technology into the classroom the teacher must be proficient at using the available technology. Integrating the computer into lessons by showing PowerPoint presentations, using video clips, or presenting computer programs that demonstrate or are used in an instructional concept demonstrates for students the utility of technology.

Allowing students the use of technology in the classroom helps them to become proficient at navigating useful technology. This may be difficult given the available amount of technology provided by the site, but creating a rotating schedule for student access to the technology or scheduling time in the computer lab is useful.

One overlooked opportunity for practice with technology is the technology students bring with them to class. Many students have technology in their pockets and purses: their smartphones. Teachers can allow students to use their phones for daily planners, calendars, reminders, simple word processing tasks, calculators, and more.

The other use of technology for students is assistive technological devices such as speech synthesizers, optical character recognition, or reading machines. This use of technology will vary based on student needs. If a teacher believes a student should have access to this technology, it is a good idea to refer the student to the student services offices for inquiries.

MOVEMENT AND SPACE

Adult education teachers have very little control over where they teach, such as the size and shape of the room. Sometimes they are placed in very strange environments and have to make the most of the situation.

When considering the physical classroom they are assigned, the first thing teachers must consider is whether they will be able to walk around the classroom freely, to ensure all students are progressing and to help individual students. They must also arrange the class so students can move around freely when needing to gather supplies or sharpen pencils or to be excused for break. Creating an environment that allows for student movement helps with student engagement. Instructional strategies which incorporate student movement are a good idea since physical activity increases neuronal metabolism and reduces stress.

Teachers who use movement to focus students must be sure to have clear expectations about student movement and clear signals for returning to seats and getting refocused.

Traditional seating arrangements in the classroom work best for a teacher-centered instructional modality. Luckily, with adult students, it is easy to rearrange the room for group work or partner work.

CONCLUSION

Classroom environment for adult learners is more about the emotional and intellectual expectations created by the teacher than about the physical space. Students thrive in a classroom environment that has clear expectations, predictable routines, and engaging practices.

POINTS TO REMEMBER

- Predictable routines allow students to focus on curriculum rather than guessing what the teacher will do next.
- Positive teacher-student interactions create a safe learning environment.
- Classroom management should focus on the behavior, not on the student.
- Adults are motivated by curriculum relevance.
- A visually stimulating environment can enhance student motivation.
- The use of technology in the classroom allows students to experience the classroom as a simulation of the workplace.
- Movement and space in the adult classroom can be fluid depending on curricular needs.

NOTES

1. Laurie Materna, *Jump Start the Adult Learner: How to Engage and Motivate Adults Using Brain-Compatible Strategies* (Thousand Oaks, CA: Corwin Press, 2007), 6–7.

2. Jeffery A. Cantor, *Delivering Instruction to Adult Learners* (Toronto: Wall & Emerson, 1992), 152.

3. Marcia Tate, *"Sit and Get" Won't Grow Dendrites: 20 Professional Learning Strategies That Engage the Adult Brain* (Thousand Oaks, CA: Corwin Press, 2004), 31–33.

4. Tate, *"Sit and Get,"* 93–96.

5. Tate, *"Sit and Get,"* 85–88.

EIGHT

Delivery of New Materials

When a person can complete a task or recall detailed information, often they will explain, "I know it by heart." Not everything learned in school is something students must know by heart, but the phrase is a clue into the best kind of teaching and learning.

The ultimate goal of any instructor is that the method of instruction be experience-centered to maximize the use of your learner's past experiences and facilitate mastery of new material.

As the instructor, it is important to pay attention to the instructional content to determine what methods best fit the material and the learner's needs. Matching these essential elements for productive learning, content, instructional methods, and learner's needs will result in the best delivery of new materials. To be able to do this, instructors must be prepared with organized lessons that have clear expectations for outcomes, a plan for appropriate grouping of students, organized materials, timed sequencing of learning stages, and time to debrief learners.

THE HOOK: TYING IT INTO WHAT THEY ALREADY KNOW

Many adults return to the classroom to "retake" classes they never mastered attending traditional school, while many sign up for classes to learn a new skill. In either case, the best way for a student to integrate new information is through tying the information to something the students already know. To do this, the teacher should develop an "anticipatory set"—a short unit that reminds students of previously learned knowledge related to the new material. This anticipatory set allows students to connect new knowledge with previous knowledge and to feel more comfortable tackling the new material. [1]

In Terry's classroom, he was struggling to help his students understand how measuring in metrics worked. He had posted bulletin boards, provided graphic organizers, and had students complete exercise after exercise. Still, when he checked for understanding, most students were still confused. Finally, he brought in dimes, dollar bills, ten dollar bills and hundred dollar bills, all from his daughter's play money.

He did a warm-up exercise on counting money in tens. Then he reviewed with the class the designation for different sizes of denominations: ones, tens, hundreds, thousands, millions, and higher. All of the students were able to complete all the tasks with no help from Terry. They were feeling confident and successful.

Then he wrote the metric system for measuring length on the board and asked students to draw comparisons with amounts of money. Jill walked to the board and began writing millimeter, centimeter, meter next to each money value and a class discussion ensued about the best designations to draw an accurate comparison. Terry sat back and let the students teach each other and felt confident that now his students had tied the new knowledge to existing knowledge. Of course, it would have been better if Terry had started the unit on metrics this way, but he would know to tie new information to existing information for future lessons.

In the adult classroom, students bring a variety of unique experiences and varying levels of background knowledge. The teacher will need to work to be able to meet the anticipatory set needs of every student. Using commonly shared knowledge such as money is an easy way to ensure all students begin with something they already know for the new learning to occur. There will be times when the teacher will not have such a commonly shared experience to use and must work to help students make these connections.

One way to be sure the student is able to tie the new information into information they already know is to allow them to make the connection through an open-ended anticipatory set. This set starts with a "highlight" of the new concept or information to be presented in the day's lesson. Then the teacher asks students when they have ever encountered the concept or information.

Posing an open-ended question about the new concept, then allowing students to reflect on it and what it reminds them of or how it relates to something else they know, gives students the latitude to make the connections they need. It is important in this situation that teachers honor all connections that students make, even if the teacher doesn't see the connection or feels the connection is not strong. By honoring all connections that students make, the teacher gives the students a head start. The student is able to build from the previous knowledge and revise later if necessary.

Many students will preface their sharing of personal experience with such phrases as "I don't know if this is right. . . ." This indicates that the student is trying to make connections but fears making a mistake in class. A teacher interested in allowing students to access prior knowledge can respond with reassurance: "I'm interested in your experience or thoughts on this. There is no wrong answer." It is important this response is sincere. If teachers express this sentiment but later explain how the student should be thinking about the topic, the teacher will create an environment where taking a risk can end with being told you were wrong, a consequence not really worth the risk.

One way for students to revise their connections, or find connections when they are at a complete loss due to lack of experience or lack of confidence, is to have other students share how they are tying the information into their previous knowledge. Group discussions of what the new concept may mean to students allows for sharing of experiences, experiences the teacher may not have experienced herself.

There may be students with no experience with the concept or information, or at least none they can think of. But when other students in the class are allowed to share their experiences, it will activate memories in the other students of their experiences with the concept. Many times in a classroom, when one student is sharing, the teacher will observe lots of nodding heads or "lights going on" for listening students.

If the day's lesson builds on previously learned information presented in the same class, the anticipatory set should be a review of the previous lesson.[2] For example, in a basic woodworking class, the lesson may be about using a miter saw for cutting angles on wood. The teacher would begin the lesson by reviewing the basic instructions for using a regular table saw, a skill all students are proficient with. By reviewing the use of the skill saw, the teacher reviews basic skills, and the lesson on using the miter saw will build on these skills.

Reviewing past skills learned in class is an easy way to set the situation for the new learning.

In order to help students to learn new information or concepts "by heart," it is imperative that a well-planned anticipatory set begin the lesson. By activating prior knowledge the teacher explicitly retrieves information from students' long-term memory and places it in their working memory. Then the teacher can show students how existing knowledge is related to the new concept.

Tying new concepts into existing knowledge facilitates what the brain wants to do: tie new learning to an existing schema. Anticipatory sets can focus either on the personal experiences of students or on the review of previously learned skills that will be useful in the new unit.

MAKING THE INFORMATION APPLICABLE TO THEIR LIVES

Another component of the delivery of new materials is to make the information applicable to the students' lives. Whether they are learning algebra or how to weld, if students cannot see how the information will benefit them, they will have a difficult time paying attention and integrating the new knowledge into their experiences.

Many teachers might assume that because a student has signed up for the class, students come with ideas about how the information is applicable to their lives and there is no need to illustrate this for students. This assumption could lead to teachers presenting lessons that have little value to students.

For example, in a basic math class Jennifer was teaching her class how to measure area. She had many students express the idea that they would never need to know how to do this and that they only wanted a grade so they could move on to the class they really wanted to take, Workplace Safety for Construction Sites. She brought up the idea of ordering carpet for a room.

"You just call the company. They come out and measure."

Jennifer wondered if they thought they might ever work in a job where *they* were "the company" who needed to do the measuring. Some students still held to the idea that they didn't need to know how to measure for area because they'd never have that job.

Jennifer asked how many students got more than one bid when ordering carpet. Few students nodded their heads. She told the story of getting a bid for carpeting and the company wrote up the bid for 200 square yards but the house was only 700 square feet and she was not getting carpet in the kitchen, dining room, or bathroom.

"What's wrong with this picture?" she asked and waited.

"The math is wrong," one student answered. Jennifer did the math on the board which showed the company was trying to charge her for 600 square feet of carpet for a 700 square foot house.

"They were trying to rip you off."

Suddenly, the lesson was very applicable to everyone's lives because Jennifer was able to tie the information to the needs of her students, the need to be treated fairly by a company.

Before a teacher plans any lesson, her initial job is to determine the needs of her students. Determining student needs can be accomplished a number of ways.[3]

Taking a class inventory of what they know and what they feel they need to know through a K-W-L chart is a quick way of getting this information. K-W-L stands for Know, Want to know, Learned. A K-W-L chart helps students reflect on the syllabus and explore what they feel are the most important lessons. It helps the teacher to recognize which lessons the students are already motivated for and which she will need to be sure to increase motivation for.

Having students complete an initial assessment that formally measures what they know and need to know allows teachers to target instruction to knowledge gaps. Since adults come to the classroom with a variety of experiences, an initial assessment helps a teacher plan meaningful learning experiences for all students while keeping in mind knowledge areas that need to be carefully reviewed or artfully expanded.

For example, in writing classes, grammar lessons can be structured as mini-lessons. Mini-lessons act as a review for those who are proficient in the grammar rules but as a corrective measure for those who are mistaking the grammar rules. The teacher can determine from writing samples which grammar rules most students are struggling with and provide lessons to practice these rules until mastery.

Teachers who are aware that many students are proficient in the new concepts, but still feel it is important to devote a lesson to the information, can make the lesson a chance for proficient students to extend their knowledge through supporting peer teaching or challenge questions.

For example, if the lesson is focused on students being able to use adverbs correctly, those students who show proficiency can have the option of working with a student who is still struggling as her "coach" or with a challenge assignment such as "Write a twenty-line poem using as many adverbs as possible." Either of these options allows proficient students to remain engaged in the lesson in a meaningful way.

When a teacher understands the needs of her students, she will want to create an instructional objective, a precise statement of what the learner will be able to do at the end of instruction. Instructional objectives are like a map to a destination. The verb in a map might be walk, drive, or bicycle and the destination might be beach, city, store, or treasure. The verb in an instructional objective might be write, design, or calculate, and the destination might be an opinion essay, a birdhouse, or the area of a room. To keep learners focused on pertinent information, referring back to the instructional objective is helpful. It reminds them of what they need to be doing to get to their destination.

If a student is following the map of the instructional objective but doesn't understand the street signs, there is a problem. Lessons must start with a review of relevant vocabulary with an explanation of why students need to know the "vocabulary" for the topic. This should be followed with time for students to create their own schema for the vocabulary.

For example, Stephanie was teaching a literacy class of second-language learners how to "read an image." The explanation included words such as "convey," "significant," and "observation." The text was written at a fourth-grade reading level, the entry level requirement for students to be in the class. Still the explanation was incomprehensible because some of the key vocabulary was unfamiliar to the students. Because of this, Stephanie spent the beginning of instructional time reviewing the pronunciation of the words, tying the words to language cognates, providing context for the words, providing student time to practice using the words in conversation, and ending with a checking of understanding.

Teachers must be sure to "upload" important vocabulary for students to ensure access to the information and concepts. By providing time for students to create a list of synonyms, create personal references (e.g., drawing a picture illustrating the meaning of the word), and practice with the unfamiliar words, teachers are ensuring all students can be successful with the lesson.

Another key element in helping students to learn the material by heart is creating a picture of the concept. Visualization engages the thalamus and amygdala portions of the brain, those areas of the brain that store emotional memories, which are the strongest memories.[4]

When a teacher shows a visual representation or has students draw their own representation, which is a kinesthetic exercise, this helps to engage areas of the brain that process concrete concepts and tie the abstract ideas to these concrete and emotional concepts. Adult brains remain strong in kinesthetic memory, so combining movement with mental and sensory rehearsal when learning new concepts makes those concepts more likely to be retained automatically.

A classroom filled with visual representations of information and concepts, whether posters, hands-on manipulatives, or virtual field trips, is visually pleasing and supports the curriculum. It is also "brain pleasing" and helps students to make strong connections with the material.

It is important that not only are concepts represented visually for students in the classroom, but that students are given the opportunity to create their own visual representations of concepts, making the information personal.

For example, in a course on healthy living, Robert has students think about how a house represents a relationship. He provides very general concepts such as the foundation representing shared experiences and the roof representing shelter from the outside, then asks students to draw two houses of their own. One house is to represent a healthy relationship and one house is to represent an unhealthy relationship. The exercise allows students to connect prior knowledge and concepts to the new information being presented in class. Once students have created posters or visual representation of the concepts, Robert allows them time to explain these concepts in their own words with the class. This verbal explanation further strengthens the concepts or increases the learning of the concept by heart.

When a teacher is presenting new information or a new concept, providing students time to see how the information is applicable to their lives is important.

PROVIDING TIME FOR REFLECTION

Many at-risk students want to move quickly through their education, not to mention a class or specific lesson. But, as the old saying goes, haste makes waste.

The brain is only able to learn seven new bits of information before needing time to move the information into long-term memory. Giving students time for this transition of information means creating situations in the classroom where they can reflect on what they are learning in order to move it into long-term memory. Effective lessons allow time for students to talk about the information, listen to the information, read about the information, and write about the information.[5]

In Martha's computer class, the lesson is on using the editing features in word processing. First, Martha has the students discuss with partners why the editing features are so important and what experience the students already have with them. Then Martha has students share their ideas out loud. When students make important points, Martha repeats them, writes them on the board, and asks students to write them down.

Finally, Martha projects a list of editing features onto a screen at the front of the class and asks students to read the directions for accessing each one. Martha has students complete a step, practice with it, show proficiency with it, then moves on to the next step. The lesson loops through talk, listen, read, and write many times during the class. When class ends, students are encouraged to go home, review their notes, and practice on personal documents to further strengthen the storing of the information into long-term memory.

The amount of reflection needed for each student to integrate the knowledge into long-term memory will depend on the student. A student's personality, family background, natural talents, physical appearance and health, system of beliefs, fears, and hopes create a cognitive appraisal that defines for him what is happening. This mental process forms the basis for the unique ways each student interprets his or her surroundings, the ways each student gives meaning to outside events, and the ways each student considers the situation he or she is encountering at school. This consideration leads to the student's feelings and behaviors in the classroom. Because of this process, it is important to provide students time for metacognitive reflection.

Metacognition, a learner's awareness of their own knowledge and their ability to understand, control, and manipulate their thinking processes, allows a student to monitor their success and challenges when learning new material.[6] Those students with good metacognition are able to retrieve memories important to the concepts being learned, are able to understand the information being communicated to them, are able to recognize when they don't understand, are able to identify which strategies to use to overcome these failures, and are able to adjust their learning in response to feedback from others.

Research shows that students with good metacognition skills are more resilient in the classroom and succeed more frequently in the classroom. Each of these discrete skills can be taught and can become automatic for all learners.

As has been reviewed, a good anticipatory set for a lesson allows students time for retrieving prior knowledge and emotional memories to connect to new information or concepts. Another concept previously reviewed, checking for understanding, allows students to assess whether they understand the information being presented. After this assessment, the teacher can help students who are lagging behind to catch up.

Providing reflection time for adult learners to develop or rely on strategies for overcoming failures is an important part of the teaching process for at-risk students. As mentioned, at-risk students often move quickly through lessons, and if they are not successful they blame something outside of themselves and give up.

Melissa kept flunking the weekly vocabulary quiz and told her teacher that she was no good at memorizing definitions. When the teacher asked her how she was studying for the quizzes, Melissa explained that she was reading over her notes each night. The teacher suggested Melissa make flash cards. Melissa stayed during break so the teacher could show her how to make the cards. The teacher also gave her instructions to run through the cards at least five times each night. On the next vocabulary quiz, Melissa was astounded at how well she did. She simply needed the right learning strategy to overcome her difficulty with learning vocabulary.

Often students are unsuccessful in certain academics because they are using a study or learning strategy that does not fit their learning style or learning strengths. By giving students time to reflect on their strategies and providing opportunities to try out new strategies, teachers provide a path to success for students who may never have experienced it in certain curricular areas.

Time to reflect on assignment feedback also allows students to monitor their own learning. When Tracy hands back written assignments, she asks students to spend ten minutes reading over the comments on the paper and then to write a page describing what they could have done differently to improve their success on the assignment. This reflection shows students how to adjust their learning based on feedback. It also steers them away from placing the blame for a low grade on something outside of them and therefore uncontrollable.

The use of student reflection time to process how they are doing with connecting new knowledge to prior knowledge, to gauge how much they understand, and to think about the teacher's feedback helps students stay motivated and focused on what they are learning.

A teacher's goal is to transfer the responsibility for monitoring progress from the teacher to the students. By allowing students a few minutes throughout the lesson to check in with their neighbor and explain what they understand, what they don't understand, and what they need to do next to successfully understand all the material, the teacher gives the students' brains time to move information learned into long-term memory and to move to the front what needs to be learned into working memory.

To promote classroom sharing of metacognition, teachers can provide sentence starters and have students share their thoughts with the class, with each other, or with the teacher. Some metacognition sentence starters might include:

"A different way to solve this problem might be . . ."

"The plan I have to work out the problem is . . ."

"What I already know about this includes . . ."

"I did a problem like this before and . . ."

Many times teachers are reluctant to allow partner work because they fear that students will go off task, talking about their weekend rather than the lesson. If students are talking about their weekend, it is usually because they have already checked in with their partner and feel like they understand the information and are prepared for the next part of the lesson. This is especially true when students have sentence stems to promote on-task classroom discussions.

Another struggle teachers have with partner work is the teacher's desire to provide all the answers. Many adult learners have struggled in school and, instead of learning the curricular content, became terrific at seeking help. It is important for students to learn to find their own mistakes or to be able to integrate feedback to adjust their new knowledge.

When students ask Michael for help, instead of reiterating the directions for completion of the assignment, Michael has those students explain to him what they do know how to complete. This allows Michael to listen to the student reflecting orally what they understand, which gives Michael the opportunity to reaffirm what students do understand and redirect where students have misunderstood.

Another great way for students to reflect on learning is through a learning journal. A learning journal is a journal where students can write about what they have learned or engage in metacognition. To get students started with a learning journal, a teacher can ask students to respond daily to the prompt "Today I learned . . ." This gives them an opportunity to cement their knowledge in the form of writing (kinesthetic) and in a way that is in their control.

Another great use for learning journals is to provide a writing prompt that asks the student to reflect on what they have learned and asks them to apply the new information and skills to a real-world situation. A student's ability to transfer the new knowledge to a familiar situation allows the student to use the new knowledge and allows the teacher to check for depth of comprehension.

For example, at the end of a lesson on reporting an incident in a public safety seminar, the teacher showed the students a video of an accident occurring in a shopping mall parking lot and asked students to write an incident report based on the skills learned in that lesson. The students will reflect on their learning while applying that learning to a new scenario. And the teacher is able to check for understanding before moving to the next set of concepts and skills to be taught.

Students should be aware that learning journals will not be graded and that the teacher will only be reading for metacognition of the new concepts. Reading learning journals is another way teachers can show students how to reflect on their learning and to prepare for upcoming lessons.

EXAMINING THE INFORMATION

When introducing new information, students must have time to examine the content from many different angles.[7] As mentioned earlier, a working knowledge of new vocabulary is foremost when learning new concepts. Students must master new vocabulary terms so they can follow the discussion of the topic. The teacher must decide what information must be mastered before introducing a concept and which skills must be taught before more complex skills are introduced. For example, in a fire rescue class, students must first be proficient with stabilizing victims before they are taught techniques for extracting victims from vehicles or high-risk situations. There are "building blocks" to learning proper rescue techniques.

In all classes in which complex skills or concepts are taught, skills must be carefully sequenced so that higher-level competencies are built upon lower-level ones.[8] For instance, mathematical learning requires not only conceptual understanding and application but also the use of strategies for problem solving. Assessment of skills and strategies needs to be ongoing.

When introducing new material, and to reinforce metacognitive manipulation of the new material, teachers can do "think alouds." "Think alouds" model for students how to make cognitive sense of the new information. They are also an excellent way for students to be presented with a visual of the new material, to hear about the new material, and to understand how to manage the new information cognitively.

For example, when teaching fact versus opinion in a basic English class, the teacher reads the text while students read along. She frequently stops and changes the tone of her voice to indicate to students that she is now sharing what she is thinking, her metacognition, with the students. For example, she may say, "Here the text uses the word 'best'; I know this term usually indicates that the sentence is an opinion. This is because 'best' is not a term usually measured but a term used to describe an opinion, such as when I say that it is the best movie." This allows students to hear and understand how proficient learners make sense of new material.

Once students have a structure for understanding new material, when teachers provide time for them to interact with this material in an un-structured way, students are able to explore and brainstorm for making personal meaning. When possible and when safety is ensured, the exploration can include manipulatives or models. This allows students to engage in the new material on a kinesthetic level, which helps with those students who learn best by "learning by heart" or when physical actions are needed to complete a task.[9] Lessons that lend themselves to manipulatives include learning to use a computer, using medical equipment, or using other equipment. Hands-on learning is implicit learning, which means that our brain is no longer creating schema but is creating movement memory.

Finally, presenting new information through metaphors, analogies, or similes can be very successful for at-risk students. Most concepts are understood only in relation to other concepts.[10] For example, when teaching the anatomy lesson on blood circulation, Charles brings in hoses and PVC pipes and starts by discussing sprinkler systems, something most of his students have some experience with. Then he compares the two or shows how one is like the other.

When presenting new information to at-risk students, being creative is the most effective manner to help them integrate the new information into prior knowledge. Most of these students were not successful in a traditional classroom that focused on lectures and tests. At-risk students will appreciate the creative approach to teaching and will be motivated by the success they experience with these alternative methods.

FEEDBACK

Finally, when introducing new material, as students are learning, appropriate feedback is important. If a student is mislearning a new concept, it is important for a teacher to catch this early and set the learner back on the correct path.

How does the teacher know if a student is mislearning or simply making an unusual connection? Asking open-ended questions such as

"Can you explain that more?" or "Can you describe the concept in another way?" will help the teacher know if the student is on the right or wrong track.

Everyone needs evaluative feedback.[11] We need to know how we are doing. Feedback is crucial for learning. Ways of providing feedback include echoing the student as confirmation of understanding the material, elaborating on the student contribution as a way of filling in the gaps of what the student knows about the concept, and explaining the concept again in a new way.

Feedback needs to exist beyond a final grade on a written assignment or test. When these are the only times students receive feedback, after the assignment is completed, they feel powerless to change their learning behaviors for improvement. Opportunities to use feedback to guide learning helps students to take risks without fearing reprisal and with assurance of being kept on the right path when new information or concepts are being taught.

For example, in a class on interpersonal communications, the instructor routinely has students role play communication scenarios to provide time for in-class coaching. Students involved in the role play are able to receive feedback immediately and retry the scenario while students observing learn from their successes and mistakes.

USING PEER SUPPORT GROUPS FOR PROCESSING

As mentioned earlier, there will be times in class when other students will be a greater resource than the teacher. This works to a teacher's advantage. Outside of the classroom, teachers are available for questions through email, but often students are able to understand information better when it is coming from their peers. Creating phone trees, email trees, or online student forums provides students the opportunity to receive peer support for processing of information.

Nancy was taking a biology class and left most nights feeling like she understood everything presented in class. But when she got home and tried to complete her homework, she was at a total loss. She emailed the teacher, but the teacher's response was just as confusing as the explanation found in the textbook. She finally called a classmate who told her, "Think of the cell membrane like your own skin. When you put on your make-up there are certain products you want to soak into your skin, to change it, and others that stay on the surface." The classmate continued explaining the concepts using shared knowledge, and Nancy returned to class the next week feeling confident.

CONCLUSION

Students learn best when they interact with the material intellectually, emotionally, and physically. Active participation through writing, partner work, and manipulatives helps retention and mastery of skills more than simple lectures and tests. A teacher's goal is to make each lesson as experience based as possible.

POINTS TO REMEMBER

- Hooking student interest to new concepts or skills is a matter of tying it to existing knowledge and experience.
- When students are aware of how skills, concepts, and information can immediately be applied to their lives, their engagement with the material increases.
- Initial assessment of student skills and knowledge helps teachers create targeted lesson plans.
- Content-specific vocabulary must be uploaded to help students comprehend new concepts.
- Visualizing concepts engages students' brains to increase retention and mastery.
- Time for reflection within lessons allows students time to integrate new knowledge into existing knowledge and experience.
- Teaching metacognition, a learner's awareness of her thinking process, is important for creating successful learners.
- Learning journals promote metacognition for students.
- Evaluative feedback helps students improve their classroom performance.
- Peer support creates a positive classroom experience for all learners.

NOTES

1. John Hollingsworth and Silvia Ybarra, *Explicit Direct Instruction: The Power of the Well-Crafted, Well-Taught Lesson* (Thousand Oaks, CA: Corwin Press, 2009), 96–97.
2. Hollingsworth and Ybarra, *Explicit Direct Instruction,* 84–88.
3. Jeffery A. Cantor, *Delivering Instruction to Adult Learners* (Toronto: Wall & Emerson, 1992) 61–62.
4. Laurie Materna, *Jump Start the Adult Learner: How to Engage and Motivate Adults Using Brain-Compatible Strategies* (Thousand Oaks, CA: Corwin Press, 2007), 79–84.
5. Materna, *Jump Start the Adult Learner,* 162.
6. Materna, *Jump Start the Adult Learner,* 94–95.
7. Hollingsworth and Ybarra, *Explicit Direct Instruction,* 163.
8. Hollingsworth and Ybarra, *Explicit Direct Instruction,* 84–88.
9. Materna, *Jump Start the Adult Learner,* 40–41.

10. Marcia Tate, *"Sit and Get" Won't Grow Dendrites: 20 Professional Learning Strategies That Engage the Adult Brain* (Thousand Oaks, CA: Corwin Press, 2004), 43–46.

11. Hendrie Weisinger, *The Power of Positive Criticism* (New York: Amacom, 2000), 3.

NINE

Explicit Teaching of Problem-Solving Skills

Students come to the classroom to attain new skills. They look to the teacher to be the expert in a field of study or a person who knows how to complete tasks and can show them how to complete those same tasks.

There is the saying that "those who can do, and those who can't teach." But every teacher knows that those who can and can show how—those are the people who can teach. This is the task of teachers for adults, the task of explaining how to solve problems in their area of expertise.

Explicit teaching or teacher-centered teaching is the most effective instructional approach to problem-solving skills. It is highly efficient because little time is wasted. The teacher-centered approach produces higher achievement among all students, including those with learning disabilities, those who are at risk, and those who are less prepared.[1]

To meet the needs of all students, a multimodal approach is best. Students have different preferred learning modes: visual, auditory, kinesthetic. By writing the assignment on the board, using visuals or pictures and diagrams, describing to students what is to be done, and providing students with objects or manipulatives, a teacher provides a learning environment that comprises all of these modes.

Teacher preparation is essential for a successful lesson on problem solving.[2] Skills must be carefully sequenced so that higher-level competencies are built on lower-level ones. For example, mathematical learning requires that conceptual understanding and application be built on knowledge of basic math facts and also requires the use of strategies for identifying the type of problem-solving skills required.

Solving problems requires that students are proficient at lower-level skills before moving on to gradually increasing levels of difficulty. Students are unable to divide numbers before they have mastered addition, subtraction, and multiplication. Likewise, all problem-solving skills require that teachers ensure students have mastered the progression of skills before moving onto more challenging concepts.

TEST STUDENT KNOWLEDGE

Knowing where to begin teaching problem solving is critical. An early assessment of student skills (known as a pretest) will ensure that teachers and students are not wasting their time practicing skills that don't require practice or are not attempting to solve problems without the necessary skills required.

The goal of a pretest is to measure a student's ability to access or retrieve stored memories with ease. A good pretest will test knowledge and facts. Simple knowledge pretests show how much students are able to rely on their memory and access to previously learned skills. A student's ability will depend on how well the material is clustered and organized in long-term memory, as well as the student's ability to use the appropriate search strategy for retrieval.

Students should have already been exposed to the concepts and facts on the pretest because the goal is not to stump students but to assess their ability to retrieve the previously learned information. During pretesting students may express frustration because they had learned the material in a previous class but are now unable to retrieve the information for the test. This demonstrates how important it is to reteach these concepts in a manner that will allow for easy retrieval for later lessons.

Problem solving requires two distinct types of knowledge: declarative knowledge, or what students know, and procedural knowledge, or what students do. A well-designed pretest will measure both of these.

Once lessons have been created to meet the needs of students and to reach the goals of the course, teachers must continue to test student knowledge in the form of checking for understanding, also known as comprehension checks. Moving on in a lesson when students have not mastered material endangers their ability to continue gaining the skills.

Checking for understanding while students are learning means the pacing of lessons needs to be interactive.[3] After the introduction of a skill or concept and student time to practice the skill or concept, teachers must check for understanding before moving on to the next concept or skill. This can be accomplished by asking random students open-ended questions, asking for thumbs up or down for a closed-ended question, or asking for students to model the use of the new information.

PROVIDE CONTEXT AND ALLOW PREDICTIONS

Before beginning any lesson, it is important to review prerequisite knowledge. By reminding students what they learned in previous lessons, teachers can demonstrate how that knowledge serves as the foundation for the upcoming lesson. For example, in a class on personal finance, a lesson on consumer credit may begin with a review of the term "disposable income" and how that fits in with an overall budget.

Providing students with a new context for using previously learned material and then allowing them to predict how to apply the knowledge to the new situation engages the student in problem solving.[4] Using the example above, once students have reviewed disposable income, they could be presented with a scenario: Their television breaks and the local store currently has special financing for purchasing televisions. The store's advertisement has a list of prices for the televisions. Students would be able to compare their monthly disposable income to the purchase price of a television, then decide if the financing would be a good idea. This exercise not only reviews the previously learned information in a real-world scenario but allows them to apply the information to a new situation and predict the best course of action. Students solve the problem of needing to purchase a new television.

Having students write down how they made their decision allows them to review the steps they went through to solve the problem.[5] When students record their process for applying the knowledge in the new context, they will be able to reflect on their problem-solving skills. They are able to examine their own process of problem solving and later in the lesson compare it to the problem-solving procedures presented in class, making revisions if necessary.

Teaching problem solving in context connects the process to schemas already present in long-term memory and builds a pathway for working with and applying the information and the skills.

TEACH TO STUDENT "GAPS"

When teaching problem solving, it is imperative that students know what problem they are learning to solve.[6] Students are made aware of this through the statement of lesson goals the teacher sets out when beginning the instructional portion of the lesson. For example, a lesson goal of "identify persuasive transitional phrases in an opinion essay and explore their impact on a reader" tells students they will solve the problem of seeing through a writer's technique to the core of an argument.

The statement of the lesson goal allows students to demonstrate what they have already mastered in the lesson plan and gives them permission to move to more difficult tasks, such as examining the impact on a reader.

As a teacher is going through the steps of solving this problem, students can demonstrate mastery or a need for more practice at each step. The lesson goal sets a clear goal for identifying and targeting student gaps in knowledge for this skill.

BREAK PROBLEMS INTO WORKABLE CHUNKS

Once students are aware of the lesson goal, breaking down the goal into manageable parts allows students to learn each step or piece of information needed, store the knowledge for retrieval for each progressive step, and build on their skills.[7]

The best way to begin to break the lesson into workable chunks is to complete a demonstration of what the solving of the problem will look like. Teachers should make explicit their own thinking process. A "think aloud" reveals to students each step required to solve a problem. Demonstrations allow for clarification of context and support kinesthetic learning.

For example, in the personal finance class, when students learned about creating a budget the teacher broke it down into manageable sections using a spreadsheet. She showed students how to track all income. Then she reviewed which costs were stable and predictable such as rent and utilities. Finally she reviewed costs of living that could be managed such as shopping and entertainment. By reviewing each chunk of creating a budget, students were able to follow along, practice with, and master each chunk before moving on to more difficult parts of managing a budget.

The added benefit of breaking a problem into workable chunks is the opportunity for interpersonal communication. Students can be paired or put in groups where they can help one another through each step. Often students who understand the teacher's directions can then translate those directions for other students into simple language everyone understands. Teachers may take for granted vocabulary unique to the problem that students often fail to comprehend.

By planning a lesson where the problem-solving skills are broken into workable chunks, the ability to continue the assessment of skills and strategies can be ongoing. A teacher can check for understanding for each chunk before moving onto the next important chunk.

USE ERRORS FOR TEACHING

As teachers break down lessons into workable chunks and check for understanding, they can use student errors as teaching opportunities.[8] Student errors are opportunities for coaching students through the process of solving the complete problem.

Students must feel safe to share their errors with the teacher, which is possible if the teacher has created a learning environment in which errors are part of the learning process. Teachers can use their own errors as examples of how to attain deeper knowledge of a subject. Also, when a teacher notices a student error, by asking for an explanation of the student's process, the teacher can reassure the student that making errors is part of having problem-solving skills.

For example, one teacher, Mary, sometimes misspells words when writing on the board. She lets the students know that she welcomes student corrections. She explains which words give her trouble and why. Often this is a great opportunity to review spelling rules and exceptions to those rules. Then she points out that she uses spellcheck for all of her important documents to be sure she has these mistakes corrected in formal documents. When Mary explains her own weaknesses, she allows for her students to also make errors in class. When she welcomes student corrections, she creates an environment that is collaborative for all.

Teachers must be careful to focus on acquisition of concepts, rather than emphasizing the correction of insignificant errors when teaching new concepts. For example, if a student is writing an explanation of how transitional phrases can affect a reader, this is not the time for the teacher to correct spelling or grammar. Or if, in a lesson on personal budgeting skills, the teacher noticed that students were making addition and subtraction errors, the teacher can let them use the calculators that are on their cell phones. These math skills should have been mastered before enrolling in the class, but now was not the time to develop them. Basic math facts were not the focus of the lesson; budgeting skills were. The important part of the lesson is the acquisition of the concept, not the details of the student attempt at demonstrating the comprehension of the skill. If students are overly concerned with details being correct, they will not be able to focus on the larger concept being taught.

Catching student errors during the acquisition of skills or concepts is best done during guided practice, a time when students are practicing the skills in workable chunks.[9] A teacher who is monitoring guided practice is given opportunities for coaching students who are struggling. Students can then demonstrate mastery during independent practice or seek specific, individual support from the teacher on their own if necessary.

Identifying errors is also a great opportunity to teach metacognition strategies or a student's ability to monitor their successful learning, to plan ahead for the next workable chunk, and to gain an awareness of learning style and strategies.

Teaching problem solving using workable chunks and student errors to inform instruction allows students to build necessary skills to complete complex problems and to integrate the new knowledge with previous learning.

QUESTIONING SKILLS

Teaching problem solving requires a bit of problem solving on the teacher's part before he even begins to teach. Solving the problem of managing the gray area between challenging students and overwhelming them can be tricky. The planning and use of questions during the lesson will help a teacher manage this challenge. [10]

There are two types of questions to utilize when teaching problem solving: direct questions and overhead questions.

Overhead questions are those questions that begin discussions, promote thinking, and elicit opinions. These questions promote metacognition including predicting, monitoring learning, planning ahead, and gauging success.

For example, questions such as "Can anyone tell me about a time when . . . ?" is an overhead question to begin discussion. It allows many students to respond and all answers are equally valid. A question such as "What might happen if . . . ?" is an overhead question to promote thinking, specifically making predictions. This question might also elicit opinions from students that may promote further discussion.

Direct questions check for understanding and help a teacher know when to move on to the next workable chunk. An example of a direct question includes "What does the acronym My Dear Aunt Sally stand for?" This question has a right and wrong answer and is meant to check for understanding. Direct questions can check for understanding of more complex concepts as well, such as "How does a cell metabolize?" In both example questions, the teacher is ensuring students have mastered the current chunk of information before moving to more complex information.

Questions lend themselves to the teaching of problem solving since all problems are solved by answering questions. [11] Teaching students to ask their own questions helps them frame a strategy for problem solving.

GENERALIZE SKILLS TO OTHER CONTEXTS

The importance of making sure the skills will remain with the student and are transferable to other subjects and situations by the end of the lesson cannot be overstated. [12] Showing students the academic importance of the problem-solving skills for not only one curricular area but others provides them an opportunity to see the skills as transferable.

For example, in the personal finance class, the teacher asked how many students would like to own a business. Many students raised their hands and the teacher led a discussion about how the budgeting skills learned today would help with budgeting for a business.

Providing examples of how the problem-solving skill has personal importance will also provide opportunities outside the classroom for students to practice the skill. Assigning homework to transfer the skill learned to an authentic, personal situation works for many classes. The independent practice for budgeting was for all students to review their personal budgets, applying the skills learned in class.

Finally, most adults return to school to change their lives beyond the classroom and to improve their occupational situations. Showing students how these skills apply in real-life situations will help students understand the importance of mastering the skill.

CONCLUSION

Teaching problem solving to at-risk adult students is critical. Their inability to solve problems may have created their at-risk situation. Teaching students to analyze context, to make predictions, to identify where they have gaps in knowledge, to break problems into workable chunks, to use good questioning skills, and to transfer the skills to other contexts will ensure a strengthening of problem-solving skills.

POINTS TO REMEMBER

- Testing student knowledge informs a teacher's lesson planning.
- Providing context for solving problems makes the skills relevant.
- Prediction of a solution to a problem allows for the teaching of explicit problem-solving skills.
- Identifying and teaching to student gaps in problem-solving skills targets instruction.
- Problem-solving skills are best taught in workable chunks.
- Good questioning skills are key to successful problem solving.
- Problem-solving skills that are transferable to other contexts have greater meaning for students.

NOTES

1. John Hollingsworth and Silvia Ybarra, *Explicit Direct Instruction: The Power of the Well-Crafted, Well-Taught Lesson* (Thousand Oaks, CA: Corwin Press, 2009), 11.
2. Hollingsworth and Ybarra, *Explicit Direct Instruction*, 199–200.
3. Hollingsworth and Ybarra, *Explicit Direct Instruction*, 46–49.
4. Ted D. E. McCain, *Teaching for Tomorrow: Teaching Content and Problem-Solving Skills* (Thousand Oaks, CA: Corwin Press, 2005), 23.
5. McCain, *Teaching for Tomorrow*, 50.
6. McCain, *Teaching for Tomorrow*, 52.
7. McCain, *Teaching for Tomorrow*, 59.
8. Hollingsworth and Ybarra, *Explicit Direct Instruction*, 36–40.

    9. Laurie Materna, *Jump Start the Adult Learner: How to Engage and Motivate Adults Using Brain-Compatible Strategies* (Thousand Oaks, CA: Corwin Press, 2007), 143–145.
    10. T. J. Fadem, *The Art of Asking: Ask Better Questions, Get Better Answers* (New York: FT Press, 2008), 57.
    11. Fadem, *The Art of Asking,* 61.
    12. McCain, *Teaching for Tomorrow,* 29.

TEN

The Use of Graphic Organizers and Other Nontraditional Teaching Strategies

Typically, adult at-risk students have struggled in school in the past. There are several reasons a student may have struggled in school. One reason is that the traditional classroom where the teacher lectures while students take notes is a learning experience designed for visual learners and auditory learners. Most at-risk students are kinesthetic learners, students who need hands-on learning. Learning situations that allow students to manipulate the information in a physical way work best for kinesthetic learners. Another reason may be that English is a second language for some students. Often, second-language learners also struggle in school because the information has been presented in a style that doesn't fit with the schemas they use for organizing information. A person's native language affects their communication style.

There are two major communication styles. The English-speaking world communicates in a linear fashion with a beginning, a middle, and an end. Unfortunately, communicators of this style only represent 5 percent of the world. The other 95 percent of the world communicate in a circular or contextual fashion. Communicators using the "circular/contextual" style circle around the point with lots of details and provide context to make the point. English speakers will usually interrupt these communicators demanding they "get to the point."[1]

If teachers of at-risk students recognize the different ways students learn and communicate and teach to student strengths, the students' ability to be successful with the content increases dramatically. Teachers must employ whatever instructional strategies are most effective for their students and reach beyond a traditional classroom structure of lecture and notes.

Research has consistently shown that information is retrieved more effectively when it is stored within a schema or network of ideas. Schemas are clusters of information on specific topics that include the general or central idea followed by related facts. Schemas are context or the information circling the main concept. To build a network, students must analyze and organize the information to be learned and teachers must connect the new information with the existing student schemas.

The use of nontraditional teaching methods helps teachers connect new content to existing knowledge and helps students store the information where it is easily retrieved for further learning. Using a variety of communication styles and kinesthetic learning — such as graphic organizers, memory devices, and music — will help students access the information and content in a manner that connects the information to existing schemas.

MIND MAPS AND WORD WEBS

Mind maps and word webs imitate the schema used by most learners.[2] By creating a circle of information or a deep context for the main concept (the center), mind maps mirror circular and contextual communicator schemas.

The most common graphic organizer in schools is probably the web (fig. 10.1). This is the organizer which places a circle in the middle with a word or concept and students draw lines out from that circle to draw new circles that contain words, phrases, or images that relate to the central circle. Then from these circles new lines and circles can form.

This graphic organizer is best used for brainstorming or discovery of all related words, concepts, and topics to a central idea. The web allows students to make connections without editing and may lead them to make connections they hadn't thought of earlier or to recognize connections to other topics previously learned. This helps create a pathway for storing the information in an existing schema.

VENN DIAGRAMS

Another graphic organizer is the Venn diagram (fig. 10.2). A Venn diagram consists of two overlapping circles with each circle representing a concept or idea. The overlapping portion represents the things the concepts have in common; the outlying areas contain the things the concepts do not share in common. This is a quick and easy graphic organizer for comparing and contrasting ideas or concepts.

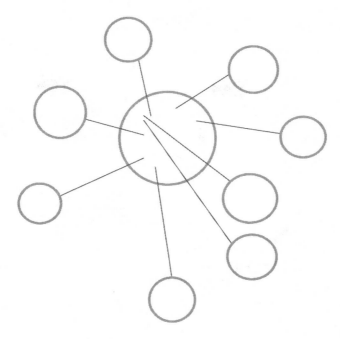

Figure 10.1.

CONCEPT MAPS

Concept maps (fig. 10.3) use the same idea of the web but with a bit more structure. Concept maps utilize boxes, circles, and lines connecting them and are arranged depending on the concept being presented.

For example, a concept map will have the main idea as a box on the top of the page. Three or four major ideas supporting the main idea appear below it with specific details for each of these ideas. This is a perfect graphic organizer for writing a traditional expository essay in which a student has to explain a main concept with supporting concepts.

Teachers can create a concept map for any concept they are teaching to students, and many are available on the Internet for teacher use. Other common examples include flow charts, family trees, and storyboards. Concept maps help students create a visual representation of an abstraction, making the concept more concrete and able to connect with an existing schema or to create a new schema for the learner.

Whatever form the concept map takes, it helps engage the learner in several ways. It forces the learner to use self-generated language and examples, it helps the learner connect the concept to prior knowledge in the generation of language and examples, and it makes the content conceptually clear through a visual representation.

Difference   Same   Difference

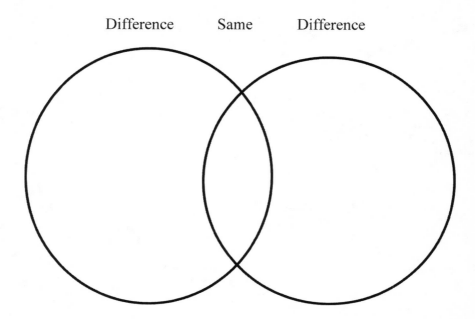

Figure 10.2.

GRAPHS AND CHARTS

Representing ideas with charts and graphs allows students to see comparisons or trends in information. These organizers for information allow students to absorb data and trends in one look.

The pie chart (fig. 10.4) is a great tool for comparing amounts. A simple pie chart is one used to represent a personal budget, but pie charts can also be created to represent the ethnic population of a geographic area or the values of a community.

When students see how a pie chart quantifies amounts, it helps them to make comparisons and to draw conclusions based on the graph. Teaching students to make their own pie charts allows them to take ownership of the format as well as teaches them to use technology.

Line graphs (fig. 10.5) are great for showing students how things change over time. Again, the graph represents data in a format that makes it easy for students to understand. Once students are familiar with a line graph, they can create their own, hopefully using technology.

Bar graphs (fig. 10.6) are great for showing comparisons.

The best use of these graphic organizers is to have students create their own. By providing graph paper and instructions or teaching them how to create them using technology, students will learn to represent

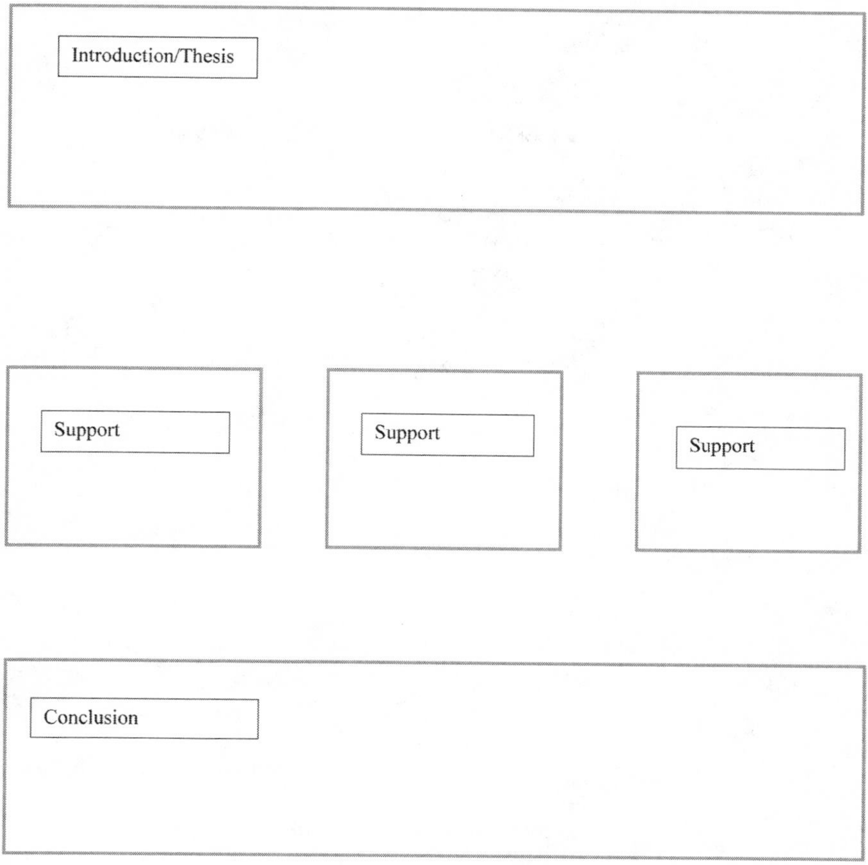

Introduction/Thesis

| Support | | Support | | Support |

| Conclusion |

Figure 10.3.

information in a way that makes it visually appealing and easily understood.

MNEMONIC DEVICES

Another nontraditional manner of helping students to integrate new knowledge into existing schemas is to use mnemonic devices or memory devices. Mnemonic devices tie new material to something already familiar.[3] They are best used to memorize a long list, new vocabulary, or information that must be memorized in a specific order. They work because the device breaks the new information into smaller segments and ties the new information to prior knowledge. This helps the brain to

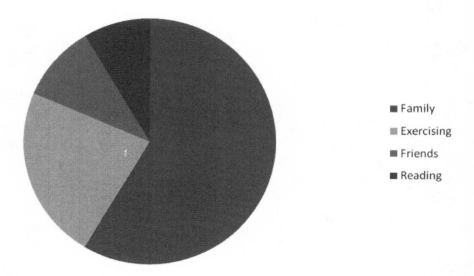

Figure 10.4.

make sense of the information with patterns or associations and to retrieve it when needed.

Examples of mnemonic devices include My Dear Aunt Sally, which
represents the basic order of operations for a math problem—Multiply,
Divide, Add, and Subtract. Another frequently used mnemonic device is
FANBOYS to remember the coordinating conjunctions—For, And, Nor,
But, Or, Yet, and So.

The best mnemonic devices are those that students create themselves.
Many times a student can remember there was a mnemonic device to
help remember something but cannot even remember the device. But
when the student has created the device, he will remember it more readi-
ly.

A teacher was helping a student remember the major contemporary
philosophies and found out the student was very involved in music. The
teacher helped the student to connect each philosophy with a musical
instrument. The student chose drums to represent deconstructionism because the cacophony of the drums can deconstruct any piece of music. He
chose the flute for emotivism because the flute seemed like the most
emotional of the instruments to him. He thought of the guitar for post-
modernism because he can make the guitar create any personal reality.
He chose the organ for poststructuralism because it makes creepy music
and the idea that a human narrative is impossible is creepy to him. Finally, the student chose the human voice to represent structuralism because
the lead singer, or conductor, creates the structure for any performance.
The student aced the test.

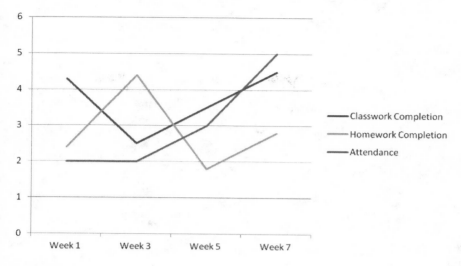

Figure 10.5.

Mnemonic devices are best when they are student generated, but teachers will want to model the use of this strategy and guide students toward the creation of their own.

POWER PICTURES

Another great way to teach a new concept is to present the concept using pictures. A person's sense of sight is his most powerful. Tying abstract concepts to a visual memory allows the brain to retrieve the information more easily.[4] A media-saturated lifestyle further emphasizes the sense of sight to make meaning of the world.

In the classroom, the teacher's goal is to create learners who will use criteria to analyze a picture and will recognize that pictures convey certain information and can be manipulated to convey specific information. Presenting pictures that can be interpreted several ways will lead to greater analysis of the picture and students justifying their interpretation with evidence from the picture.

Pictures are an important teaching strategy for teaching reading comprehension. Proficient readers create pictures in their heads of what they are reading, but many at-risk students have never been very good at this. By presenting concepts using pictures, students learn to create pictures in their heads that tie the information to a memory. Having students draw a picture of what they have read cements for them what has happened in the reading.

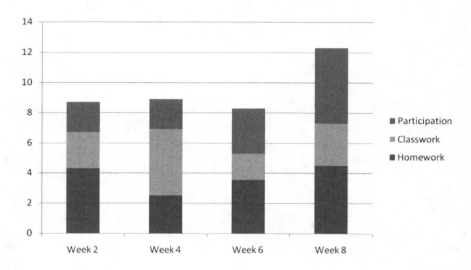

Figure 10.6.

Making students responsible for presenting their ideas in pictures powerfully cements in their brains what they have learned. PowerPoint presentations are a wonderful way for students to utilize this technique.

MUSIC: MELODY, BEAT, AND HARMONY

Another nontraditional way of connecting information with students' prior knowledge is through the use of music.

There is a great deal of research that shows that playing certain music enhances the brain's ability to focus and concentrate.[5] Song lyrics are memorable, and one reason for this is that rhyme aids memory. Nursery rhymes use this premise to teach children to count and to learn their ABCs. Those who can remember the television show *Happy Days* will remember Fonzie learning anatomy through the recitation of a song. Likewise, teachers are often amazed how students who fail to remember their multiplication tables can remember the lyrics to so many songs.

Using music to connect new ideas for students may prove difficult for teachers who are not musically inclined but may be a wonderful student assignment for those students who are. Another option is to use popular songs that illustrate concepts. A teacher reviewing diction in her English class enjoyed bringing in pop music that misused grammar. She had her class analyze the song, having students correct the grammar and do a karaoke-type assignment with the corrections.

Another use of music is to use well-known songs with new lyrics to explain the new concepts. Joann uses folk songs like "Santa Claus Is

Coming to Town" to teach characteristics of metals in her chemistry class. The options are only as limited as the class's creativity.

Properties of Metals
Chorus:
You better remember
You better not forget
The properties of metals
Are important, I'll bet
The properties of all the metals.
Verse One:
They're shiny and have luster
They're hard and malleable too
They can be stretched into wire
Ductile, to me and you . . . Oh
Chorus
Verse Two:
As conductors, they are the very best
1, 2, 3 valence electrons too . . .
When some form colored compounds
Could be red, orange, green, or blue
Chorus
Verse Three:
Metals lose their outer electrons
Whenever they form compounds
And when they make a cation
They are positively charged.

Music helps many nontraditional learners to create a schema for the new concepts and makes class fun.

CONCLUSION

At-risk students have failed in schooling many times because they are unable to learn in traditional ways. By presenting curriculum using nontraditional strategies, students will be able to make the connections necessary to learn the new information. If teachers of at-risk students recognize the different ways students learn and communicate and teach to student strengths, the students' ability to be successful with the content increases dramatically. Teachers must have the most effective instructional strategies to reach these students, strategies that reach beyond the traditional classroom structure of lecture and notes.

POINTS TO REMEMBER

- At-risk students are more successful in classrooms that engage them in nontraditional methods of learning.

- Mind maps and word webs mimic contextual schemas for remembering and retrieving information.
- Venn diagrams visually represent the comparison of ideas or things.
- Concept maps can be created to visually represent complex ideas.
- Students who understand and can generate graphs and charts are better equipped to process complex data.
- Mnemonic devices take advantage of student experiences and prior knowledge.
- Pictures and visual narratives help adult brains in making sense of information.
- The beat, melody, and harmony of music enhance the brain's ability to remember and retrieve information.

NOTES

1. Janet M. Bennett, *Values, Cultures, and Conflicts* (Oregon: The Intercultural Communications Institute, 2008), 3.

2. Marcia Tate, *"Sit and Get" Won't Grow Dendrites: 20 Professional Learning Strategies That Engage the Adult Brain* (California: Corwin Press, 2004), 23–26.

3. Tate, *"Sit and Get"* (California: Corwin Press, 2004), 49–52.

4. Laurie Materna, *Jump Start the Adult Learner: How to Engage and Motivate Adults Using Brain-Compatible Strategies* (California: Corwin Press, 2007), 29–31.

5. Tate, *"Sit and Get"* (California: Corwin Press, 2004), 60.

ELEVEN

Group Processing and Cooperative Learning Strategies

When asked what their favorite part of school was as a child, most at-risk students will identify recess or summer break. But upon closer investigation, the teacher will find that students enjoy the ability to choose their activities, like to choose whom to complete the activity with, and prefer a low level of stress involved with the activity.

Likewise, instruction and support are most effective when students are proactive and able to participate in identifying personally meaningful and realistic goals. Success in school and beyond depends not only on the quality of the instruction but on the individual's ability to sustain motivation, persistence, and effort in the courses of their education.

A returning student told his teacher how much he disliked school on the first day of class. Instead of asking him why, the teacher asked if there was anything about his school experience he did like. "I ran cross country and track." Immediately the teacher pointed out how the qualities required to be successful in running were the same qualities needed to be successful in her class: determination, persistence, and motivation. The student remained skeptical that he would like the class, but the teacher was convinced he would be successful now that she knew he had the qualities needed for success.

New research emphasizes the idea of lessons that follow the "I do, we do, you do" model. In this model, the teacher demonstrates the skills, then the class practices together to ensure proficiency, and finally students are allowed to complete the task on their own. "On their own" often means on a team. Rarely in today's world does anyone complete anything alone. Working together, focusing on each team member's strengths, provides a stronger end product and enhances the students' experience by engaging students in pro-social activities within the class.

By creating a nurturing environment that gives students choice, autonomy, and appropriate levels of stress, the use of group process teaching or cooperative learning strategies helps to engage at-risk learners.[1]

PEER TEACHING

When using the methods for identifying student gaps in knowledge, teachers will also identify student expertise. As mentioned previously, often students will learn more from each other than from the teacher because students share a similar, less technical vocabulary and can draw on shared comparisons and analogies that the teacher may not be familiar with. The use of peer teaching takes advantage of all of these positive elements in the classroom.

Peer teaching, or having a student teach other students, works well when information needs to be summarized or methods need to be demonstrated.[2] Allowing students to summarize information accesses a student friendly vocabulary while focusing on key conceptual points. A student summary also allows the teacher to chime in as a coach or mentor to fill in or expand ideas. A student demonstration allows the teacher to describe the demonstration so students see the process and hear about the process.

In a basic algebra class, Mary has her students work out problems on the board. Many other teachers think this is "old school" and a waste of classroom time, but an observer will witness magic happening. Mary hovers nearby and talks the problem-solving skills through. She will narrate the student's progress with comments like "Notice that Teri is multiplying first, the first step in any multistep math problem." Students get to see another student demonstrate how to complete the problem and hear the teacher complete a "think aloud." The added bonus is the student at the board gets positive reinforcement.

Another great use of peer teaching is reciprocal teaching. In reciprocal teaching, each student must become an expert in one area and then is responsible for teaching that area to the other students. Again, this frees up the teacher for monitoring progress, coaching, and expanding on information when appropriate.

Peer teaching also allows for students to negotiate meaning when learning a new concept. When integrating new information with existing schemas, often there needs to be some adjustment of the understanding of the concept. An explanation from peers, who are less threatening than the teacher, gives students the room to explore how the concept fits in with existing knowledge and schemas and for refinement of these ideas to occur.

In a class on private security, all students must be certified in first aid. After the pretest, the instructor identified which students were already proficient in first aid skills, then set up centers for the students to rotate through, placing a proficient student in charge of each center. This allowed the proficient students to further enhance their own knowledge of the first aid technique through explaining it to others. And it allowed the teacher to roam the class and coach where necessary. Peer teaching allows for all students to extend their present knowledge.

ROLE PLAYS

Role plays are similar to peer teaching in that students get to take on the role of the teacher and help other students understand new concepts. But role plays extend this experience by allowing students to solidify their own understanding of a concept. Because role plays are simulations, they increase meaning for students, allow for a transfer of knowledge from conceptual understanding to personal understanding, and are highly motivating for most students.[3]

In the private security class, after all students have demonstrated proficiency in first aid techniques, the teacher places students in groups of three and presents them with a "victim" they must respond to. The role play allows students practice at applying their skills in a simulated life situation.

The most common role play is the idea of a student taking on the personality of another person to act out scenes either from a reading selection or a scenario pertinent to the concept being taught. This type of role play allows students to play being personally invested in the ideas presented and to have to convince others of the meaningfulness of the ideas.

In a class on Native American anthropology, the teacher assigns students the roles of chiefs of different tribes. These "chiefs" first give a speech to the class about their priorities for their tribe, then participate in a "meeting" to discuss cooperation among the tribes. By using this role play, the students engage in dialogue about values and the cultures of the tribes. This kinesthetic, participatory exercise helps them to understand the history of the tribes they are representing and of all the tribes.

Another use of role play is to have students play the role of storyteller where they tell the class a story about the concept being presented in class. The reason most children's books are written in the form of stories is that the human brain remembers stories better than disconnected ideas or concepts. By putting students in charge of creating the stories to be told, they become personally involved in the story and the telling, cementing the concepts and ideas into their brains.

In an art appreciation class, for a mid-semester presentation, all students are given a group of historically relevant art pieces that they must present to the class using a narrative about the significance of the pieces and their relevance to each other. Students often take on the persona of a narrator or art curator, but more creative students may take on the persona of an historical personality for the presentation. The role plays allow students to make narrative sense of the art.

Another type of role play is for students to pantomime ideas and concepts presented in class. Pantomime requires students to use their bodies to become the concept and is kinesthetic. Plus it's fun.

Playing a game of charades, in groups so there is group processing of information and students can work together, allows students to have fun with the concepts while integrating them into their knowledge base. In an introduction to chemistry class, the major concepts students must understand are the elements of the periodic table. By assigning students an element to pantomime, they learn the elements in an interactive, engaging, and fun way.

Finally, having students create a television commercial and play the role of a reporter is an engaging method of teaching class concepts. This is great fun if audiovisual equipment is used to present the commercials in class.

GROUP PROCESSING OF INFORMATION

As reviewed in this book, students will often learn more from each other than from the teacher. The role of the teacher in this situation is to set the course, act as the expert or coach when needed, and allow students to teach each other. Setting up a classroom that allows for group processing of information helps students to learn from each other.[4]

Group processing is different from peer teaching, which is not always appropriate. Sometimes no students have the knowledge base to peer teach, and explicit teaching (which is teacher directed) is the best way to ensure learning. In these cases, group processing is a way to gain the benefits of peer teaching in a more traditional, teacher-directed lecture format. Group processing takes place after the teacher has completed her initial lesson and is intended to ensure that students are integrating the new knowledge into existing knowledge, understanding the information correctly, placing it in the correct schema for easy retrieval, and making personal connections with the information so it is meaningful beyond the classroom.[5]

For example, in a basic geography class, after the unit on desert climates, the teacher places students in groups for a "desert survival" exercise. Students are given a scenario where they have crashed in the desert with a list of supplies and tools. The group must rank each supply and tool in order of importance to their survival. The exercise generates a great deal of discussion about what the students just learned about desert climate and survival in the desert.

Group processing of information is not simply allowing for class or group discussions but is also an opportunity for students to interact with each other about the information in a structured, teacher-directed manner. It uses open-ended tasks, like the desert survival activity, that allow students to express opinions about the information or concepts and to speculate about how the information is important to the coursework.

An important part of group processing is to give students tools to interact appropriately within the group. For example, students should be given sentences or questions to use for clarification purposes or for negotiating meaning. Teaching students to ask, "Can you tell me what you mean by that?" rather than saying, "No, that's wrong" promotes positive group interaction.

Teachers can use sentence stems to stimulate discussion in group processing. Some examples of group interaction sentence stems include:
"In my opinion . . ."
"What do you mean by that?"
"I agree with you because . . ."
"I disagree with you because . . ."
"Could you explain that in a different way?"

As a group processing unit ends, teachers may want to assign study projects or action projects in which students apply the knowledge gained in the classroom to a community situation.

In a public safety class, the teacher assigned the class to choose one major intersection in their community that they felt needed a stoplight. Each group had to identify an intersection, collect data on the intersection about its safety, then propose how the stoplight would increase public safety. At the end of the unit, each group made a presentation to the class, just as they would present to a city council. The project allowed students to complete research, apply the knowledge gained in class, and understand their own potential to change public policy.

Group processing of information is especially important for at-risk students in that it promotes pro-social interactions, helps students to navigate new information with other students, and allows for student choice and interaction.

COOPERATIVE LEARNING STRATEGIES

When cooperative learning is mentioned in a class, most students groan. Some students conjure up past experiences where they had to do all the work while other students got credit for the assignment. Others recall working with students who were uncompromising or control freaks. Yet teachers continue to use these strategies in class because they do emulate the expectations of most occupations and provide a rich environment for learning.

The key to successful cooperative learning strategies is structure. Teachers must be sure that they have planned for the cooperation to take place, have modeled for students what this cooperation will look like, and have practiced the cooperation strategy in a low-challenge setting.[6]

Trish loves to use an exercise that she calls "Send a Problem" in her early childhood education class. On the front of several envelopes she pastes a problem scenario. Each group gets an envelope and must develop a solution to the problem which they place inside the envelope so other groups cannot see their response.

Once all groups have responded to all the scenarios, they pull out the solutions and rank them from best to worse. Then students present their results to the class. This structured activity promotes group problem solving, recognizing diverse solutions, and prioritizing solutions.

Setting up cooperative learning groups can work either with homogenous groupings or with heterogeneous groupings. A homogenous grouping puts students with common background, language, or skill levels together. This method is especially effective with students who are second-language learners; they can help each other with translations of information, often their schemas are similar, and they are able to help each other integrate the information into existing knowledge.

For example, the cooperative learning strategy called "jigsaw" works well with homogeneous groupings. If each team member becomes an expert in an area, say reads one section of a chapter in the textbook, then she can share that knowledge with the rest of the group and each member shares with her. This allows students to help each other with the workload.

Heterogeneous grouping works when you want each student to contribute in a unique way with their unique talents or learning style. This requires that the learning outcome be broad enough to engage all learners in making meaning of the concepts and in creating a product to contribute to the group's project.

For example, Robert uses group posters in his healthy living class. He creates groups that include a student with artistic ability, one with good handwriting, one with good editing skills, and one with good summarizing skills. This helps the group to create a well-rounded project.

Cooperative learning for project or problem-based instruction allows students to connect concepts to real-life situations and emulates expectations in the workplace.[7] To be successful, the group identifies each person's skills, divides the work up according to strengths, and has a person in charge of the final product just like in the workplace.

CLASS PRESENTATIONS

Class presentations tie in all the nontraditional instructional techniques discussed in this book and help teach at-risk students important skills for making presentations in front of an audience. When class presentations are done as cooperative learning projects, it creates a more complex learning experience.

Class presentations require planning, especially when the presentations are to be completed as a group. Just as when students are engaged in cooperative learning groups, group presentations work best if students divide the work into roles for completion. One student can be in charge of each portion of the presentation. Or, conversely, one student can be in charge of one aspect of the entire presentation, such as handouts, audiovisual, and speaking. These are just two of the methods to help students organize group presentations. Having clear roles for the presentations will help students be successful.

At-risk students rarely enjoy presenting to an audience, especially at school, but presentations help build speaking skills and confidence for beyond the classroom.

CONCLUSION

Group work for at-risk students is important because it gives the feel of recess or play time. Creating a nurturing environment that gives students choice in the use of group process teaching or cooperative learning strategies helps to engage at-risk learners

POINTS TO REMEMBER

- Using group processing or cooperative learning strategies promotes engagement for at-risk students.
- Peer teaching of basic curricular concepts takes advantage of positive student interactions within a classroom.
- Role plays are simulations of the curriculum that increase personal meaning for students.
- Group processing of information is an opportunity for students to interact in creating a deeper understanding of the curriculum.
- Cooperative learning strategies must be practiced in low-challenge situations and must be structured to enhance student engagement.
- Class presentations provide a safe environment for students to practice being in front of an audience.

NOTES

1. Marcia Tate, *"Sit and Get" Won't Grow Dendrites: 20 Professional Learning Strategies That Engage the Adult Brain* (Thousand Oaks, CA: Corwin Press, 2004), 69–74.

2. Samuel A. Kirk, James J. Gallager, and Nicholaus J. Anastasiow, *Educating Exceptional Children* (New York: Houghton Mifflin, 2003), 240.

3. Tate, *"Sit and Get,"* 75–78.

4. Tate, *"Sit and Get,"* 69–74.

5. Laurie Materna, *Jump Start the Adult Learner: How to Engage and Motivate Adults Using Brain-Compatible Strategies* (Thousand Oaks, CA: Corwin Press, 2007), 42.

6. Elizabeth F. Barkley, K. Patricia Cross, and Claire Howell Major, *Collaborative Learning Techniques: A Handbook for College Faculty* (San Francisco: Jossey-Bass, 2004), 72.

7. Barkley et al., *Collaborative Learning Techniques,* 12–16.

Index

acculturation, 28
acetylcholine, 23
ADD. *See* attention deficit disorder
ADHD. *See* attention deficit hyperactivity disorder
aging, brain and, 36–37
alcohol, 24
Amada, Gerald, 46
America's Perfect Storm, 7
amphetamines, 24
analogies, 77
anticipatory set, 67, 69, 74
antisocial associates, 30
antisocial attitudes and values, 29–30
antisocial personality, 29
antisocial tendencies, 17
associates, antisocial, 30
at risk, defined, 2
attention deficit disorder (ADD), 13–14
attention deficit hyperactivity disorder (ADHD), 13–14
attitudes: antisocial, 29–30; of teacher, 61
attribution theory, 18
auditory processing disorder, 16–17
authority, 33, 50
autism, 5

background knowledge, 52, 68
bar graphs, 92, 96
basal ganglia, 36
basic behavior modification theory, 47
basic needs, 44
beats, 96–97
behavior: acculturation and, 28; disorders, 17–18; misbehavior, 46; modeling, 45; modification theory, 47; off-task, 1–2. *See also* criminogenic behavior
Berlin, Rudolf, 15

biological needs, 44
blaming, pattern of, 32
blood-brain barrier, 22
brain, 35, 40, 52; adult experiences and, 37–38; aging and, 36–37; areas of, 35–36; capacity, 35; chemical abuse and, 23; communication, 21–22; dominance, 36; lobes of, 35; meaning and, 51; new materials and, 73; plasticity of, 35, 37; reflection and, 39; routine and, 57; stem, 35, 38
brainteasers, 58
breaks, 45, 49, 59
building blocks, 76
bulletin boards, 57
Bureau of Justice Statistics, vi, 3

caffeine, 22
California Department of Corrections and Rehabilitation., vi
CCARTA Summer Institute, 7
central nervous system, 10
cerebellum, 36
cerebral cortex, 35
challenge, 53–54
charades, 102
charts, 92
chemical abuse: learning and, 25–26; long-term effects of, 23–24; short-term effects of, 22–23. *See also* drugs
children: family dysfunction and, 30–31; marshmallow test and, 31; of students, 3
chronic illnesses, 24
circular/contextual style of communication, 89
clarifying questions, 48, 59
class discussions, 39, 52, 69

classroom environment, 57, 65; motivation and, 60–62; movement and, 64; predictable routine and, 57–60; space and, 64; technology and, 63–64; visuals and, 62–63
cocaine, 24
cognitive ability, 10
cognitive functioning, 11
communication: brain, 21–22; styles, 89
communication disorders, 14; auditory, 16–17; visual processing, 14–15
concept maps, 91, 93
context, 83; generalizing skills to, 86–87
contextual/circular style of communication, 89
cooperative learning strategies, 99–100, 103–104, 105; peer teaching, 100–101; presentations, 105; role plays, 101–102
Coping with Misconduct in the College Classroom (Amada), 46
crime: family history of, 31; poverty and, 6
criminal identity, 30
criminal justice center, 3
criminal thinking, 29, 32–33
criminogenic behavior, 28–29; antisocial associates and, 30; antisocial attitudes and values, 29–30; antisocial personality, 29; criminal thinking and, 32–33; family dysfunction and, 30–31; problem solving, poor, 32; self-control, poor, 31
culture: acculturation, 28; homogeneous, 28; of poverty, 6–7; values and, 28

decision-making skills, 13
declarative knowledge, 82
deinstitutionalization, 5
demographics, 3
depressants, 22
de-stressing, 45
differentiation, 61
direct questions, 86
disabilities. *See* learning disabilities
discussions, 39, 52; group, 69

distractions, eliminating, 62
dopamine, 23
drugs: brain communication and, 21–22; chemical abuse, effects of, 22–24; learning and, 25–26; PAWS and, 25; prevalence of, 21; withdrawal from, 24; *See also specific drugs*
dyscalculia, 16
dysgraphia, 15–16
dyslexia, 15
dyspraxia, 16

education: parolee, v; public, 28
emotions, 44–48; managing, 47; positive, 38
emotional adolescents, v
emotional intelligence, 47
emotional memory, 38
engagement, 9
entitlement, 32
environment: learning disabilities and, 11; risk-free, 57. *See also* classroom environment
epinephrine, 23
errors, 84–85
Escalante, Jaime, 54
evaluative feedback, 78
evidence-based instructional practices, 1
executive functions, of brain, 22
explicit teaching, 81

family dysfunction, 30–31
feedback, 47, 49; evaluative, 78; new materials and, 77–78; positive, 54; reflection and, 74
flow, 38
A Framework for Understanding Poverty (Payne), 6
frontal lobes, 35

GABA, 23
gaps, 83–84
generalizing skills, 86–87
glass ceiling, 43
graphs, 92
graphic organizers, 89–90, 97–98; charts, 92; concept maps, 91, 93;

graphs, 92; mind maps, 90; mnemonic devices, 93–95; music, 96–97; power pictures, 95–96; Venn diagrams, 90, 92

gray matter, 35

groups: discussions, 69; homogeneous grouping, 104; interviews, 10; peer support, 78

group processing, 99–100, 105; of information, 102–103; peer teaching, 100–101; presentations, 105; role plays, 101–102

hands-on learning, 77

harmony, 96–97

hidden disabilities, 10

hidden rules, 7

highlights, 68

hippocampus, 36

homogeneous culture, 28

homogeneous grouping, 104

hook, 67–69

humor, 62

identity, criminal, 30

"I do, we do, you do" model, 99

illness: chronic, 24; mental, 5

impulse control, 31

incarceration, likelihood of, 2

initial assessment, 71

institutionalization, 5

instructional objectives, 71

instructional strategies routines, 58

integration, 50

intellectual adolescents, v

intelligence, 10–11; emotional, 47

intelligence quotient (IQ), 10; dyslexia and, 15

interaction, 61; pro-social, 103

interviews, group, 10

IQ. *See* intelligence quotient

jigsaw, 104

journals, learning, 75–76

kinesthetic exercises, 72

Koutsenok, Igor, 7

K-W-L chart (Know, Want to know, Learned), 70

language, 10; appropriate, 7; modeling, 45; oral, 16; second-language learners, 89. *See also* communication disorders

learned helplessness, 18

learner-generated posters, 63

learning: drugs and, 25–26; hands-on, 77; journals, 75–76; reciprocal, 100; styles, 12. *See also* cooperative learning strategies

learning disabilities, 3–4, 9; ADD and ADHD, 13–14; asking about, 12; assessing for, 12; auditory processing disorder, 16–17; behavior disorders, 17–18; biological, 11; central nervous system and, 10; communication disorders, 14; dyscalculia, 16; dysgraphia, 15–16; dyslexia, 15; dyspraxia, 16; environmental factors of, 11; intelligence and, 10–11; planning and, 11; range of, 9; success and, 10; visual processing disorder, 14–15

left-brain dominance, 36

left-handedness, 36

lesson-timing routines, 59

line graphs, 92, 95

literacy classrooms, 58

long-term memory, 37, 73, 73

lyrics, 96

management of at-risk adult learners, 43, 55; challenge and, 53–54; emotions and, 44–48; honoring experiences, 50–52; misbehavior and, 46; support and, 53–54; timing and, 48–50

marshmallow test, 31

Maslow's hierarchy of needs, 44

math facts, 16

meaning, 51; negotiating, 100

melody, 96–97

memory: emotional, 38; long-term, 37, 73, 73; stress and, 37

mental hospitals, 5

mental illness, 5

metacognition, 73–74, 75

metaphors, 77

methamphetamines, 24
middle brain, 36
mind maps, 63, 90
mini-lessons, 71
misbehavior, 46
mnemonic devices, 93–95
motivation, 50, 60–62
movement, 64
music, 96–97

National Center for Education
    Statistics, vi
National Institute on Drug Abuse, 21,
    26
needs, 44
neurotransmitters, 21, 23
new materials, 67, 79; applicability to
    life and, 70–73; examining, 76–77;
    feedback and, 77–78; hook, 67–69;
    peer support groups and, 78;
    reflection and, 73–76
non-apparent disabilities, 10
nontraditional teaching strategies,
    89–90, 97–98; charts, 92; concept
    maps, 91, 93; graphs, 92; mind
    maps, 90; mnemonic devices, 93–95;
    music, 96–97; power pictures, 95–96;
    Venn diagrams, 90, 92
norepinephrine, 23
nursery rhymes, 96

occipital lobes, 35
off-task behavior, 1–2
open-ended prompts, 48
open-ended questions, 68, 77
optimism, 33
oral language, 16
out-of-class routines, 60
out-the-door ticket, 58
overhead questions, 86

packing up routines, 58
pantomime, 102
parietal lobes, 35
parolee education, v
PAWS. *See* post acute withdrawal
    syndrome
Payne, Ruby K., 6
peer support groups, 78

peripherals, 63
personal experience, 68
personality, antisocial, 29
physical tasks, 16
physiological needs, 44
pictures, power, 95–96
pie charts, 92, 94
planning, 11
plasticity, of brain, 35
population, demographics of, 3
positive emotions, 38
positive feedback, 54
positive tone, 45
post acute withdrawal syndrome
    (PAWS), 25
post traumatic stress disorder (PTSD),
    17
poverty, culture of, 6–7
power pictures, 95–96
PowerPoint presentations, 96
predictions, 83
preparation, of teachers, 81
presentations, 105; PowerPoint, 96
pretests, 82
primal brain, 38
problem solving, 81, 87; context and,
    83; errors and, 84–85; gaps and,
    83–84; generalizing skills and,
    86–87; poor, 32; predictions and, 83;
    questioning skills and, 86; testing
    student knowledge, 82; workable
    chunks and, 84
procedural knowledge, 82
processing disorders: auditory, 16–17;
    visual, 14–15
pro-social interactions, 103
psychological diagnoses, 17–18
PTSD. *See* post traumatic stress
    disorder
public education, 28

questions: clarifying, 48, 59; direct, 86;
    open-ended, 68, 77; overhead, 86
questioning skills, 86

reciprocal learning, 100
reflection, 49; brain and, 39; feedback
    and, 74; new materials and, 73–76
rehabilitation, vi, 8

relevance, of material, 61
right-brain dominance, 36
right-handedness, 36
risk-free environment, 57
role models, teachers as, 45, 46
role plays, 101–102
routine, 48; brain and, 57; instructional strategies, 58; lesson-timing, 59; out-of-class, 60; packing up, 58; predictable, 57–60; wait-time, 59

safety, 53
safe zone, 45
sarcasm, 62
SAT. *See* Scholastic Aptitude Test
scaffolding, 4
schemas, 90
Scholastic Aptitude Test (SAT), 10
schools, 28
second-language learners, 89
self-concept, 54
self-control, poor, 31
self-dialogue, 59
self-regulation, 13
serotonin, 23
similes, 77
situational approach, 28
smartphones, 64
smoking, 24
socialization, 29
socioeconomic growth, 7
song lyrics, 96
space, 64
Stand and Deliver (movie), 54
Stanford University, 31
stimulants, 22, 22, 24

stress, 45; dealing with, 52; memory and, 37; PTSD, 17; reduction techniques, 51; smoking and, 24
substance abuse, v; criminal behavior and, 33. *See also* drugs
Summer Institute, CCARTA, 7
super optimism, 33
support, 53–54
surveys, 12

teacher-centered teaching, 81
technology, 63–64
temporal lobes, 35
thalamus, 36
think alouds, 76, 84
thinking, 11, 17; criminal, 29, 32–33; reflection, 39
timing, 48–50
tobacco, 24
tough sentencing, vi
transactional approach, 28

values, 28; antisocial, 29–30
Venn diagrams, 90, 92
verbal mediation, 59
visitors, students as, 8
visuals, 62–63
visualization, 72
visual processing disorder, 14–15
vocabulary, 71–72

wait-time routine, 59
withdrawal, 24; PAWS, 25
word webs, 90, 91
workable chunks, 84
writing, 15

About the Author

Diane Mierzwik was a Southern California program coordinator for Contra Costa County Office of Education's California Department of Corrections and Rehabilitation program. In her eighteen years of teaching, she has had experience with first through twelfth graders. She has been the gifted and talented education coordinator, leadership team member, department head, and a mentor teacher. She has completed the Inland Empire Writing Project and served as a language arts consultant for the California Language Arts Project. She is also the author of several books and articles, most notably *Quick and Easy Ways to Connect with Students and Their Parents* and *Classroom Record Keeping Made Simple: Tips for the Time-Strapped Teacher* available from Corwin Press. Her website is www.dianemierzwik.net.